NEXT LEVEL
LIVING

RICH ROGERS
"DR. RICH"

Charisma
HOUSE
A STRANG COMPANY

NEXT LEVEL LIVING by Rich Rogers
Published by Charisma House
A Strang Company
600 Rinehart Road
Lake Mary, Florida 32746
www.charismahouse.com

Cover design: studiogearbox.com
Executive Design Director: Bill Johnson

Library of Congress Cataloging-in-Publication Data:

Rogers, Rich.
Next level living / Rich Rogers. -- 1st ed.
p. cm.
Includes bibliographical references.
ISBN 978-1-59979-197-5
1. Christian life. 2. Spiritual formation. I. Title.

BV4501.3.R663 2008
248.4--dc22

                                2007043823

First Edition

08 09 10 11 12 — 9 8 7 6 5 4 3 2 1
Printed in the United States of America

DEDICATION

To my precious church family at Free Chapel: you all are amazing. Thank you for your encouragement and prayers. Twenty-one days every January—we can move mountains with that kind of faith! And for my pastor, Jentezen Franklin, I could never repay all you have poured into me week in and week out. I pray you see parts of yourself in this book.

To my beautiful wife and four wonderful daughters, my teachers, mentors, and partners in the journey. I write the text, but we all do the work. Together, we will see the Lord change the world one million souls at a time!

CONTENTS

SECTION 5: THE GREAT AWAKENING—A CALL TO ARMS

SECTION 6: FALL IN

FOREWORD

AS I TRAVEL ALL ACROSS THE NATION AND AROUND THE WORLD to preach, I have found that night after night, the altars are filled with people responding to one of three calls from God on their lives. Some are seeking salvation for the first time, and some have fallen away or grown cold in their walk and are compelled to rededicate their lives to Christ. Then there is always a third group of people who are saved, love the Lord, and are faithful in their walk, yet they sense God calling them to something more—another level. They are responding to the voice of the Holy Spirit calling them to a higher place. I believe that *Next Level Living* was written for this third group of folks.

What Dr. Rich has done in *Next Level Living* is connect this third group of folks to a five-step pattern found all through Scripture that walks each reader through the process God has used for centuries in the lives of those He has called to a divine purpose. I have found in my own church that the pathway to leadership leads through places that don't look like a path to purpose and ministry if you look with physical eyes only. Many get discouraged and give up when the Lord doesn't propel them immediately to that vision they see in their mind. For every great character in the Bible, there was a gap between the call and the actual time that their call came to fruition. It is in this gap that many well-meaning men and women of God grow faint, get discouraged, and give up.

We must be willing to submit ourselves to the Master Potter's wheel and allow the Lord to mold us and shape us by any means He chooses. *Next Level Living* teaches the reader to recognize the hand of God in this process. In the past two years, Dr. Rich has taught this process to hundreds of folks in our church with incredible results. Testimony after testimony gives us evidence of the effectiveness of the concepts found in *Next Level Living*.

Lastly and most importantly, *Next Level Living* makes the case for the urgency of the hour we are in. Dr. Rich walks the reader through the historical and biblical account of last days' prophecy to show us the incredible age we are living in on the brink of what could be the greatest harvest ever known on Earth—the End-Time harvest and the latter rain.

Next Level Living is a book you will find hard to put down. It has changed the lives and perspectives of hundreds in our own church, and it will do the same for you.

—Jentezen Franklin

INTRODUCTION

I BELIEVE WITH ALL MY HEART THAT THE LORD HAS GIVEN ME A message to give to Christians and churches in America. It is a message of warning and instruction, but it is also a message of hope and promise. The urgency is of utmost importance as Christians all across this great country are flooding aisles of churches, seeking hope, restoration, and a plan for their lives. God has made all three available to those who will stop, listen, and then live at the next level.

What is the next level? In the physical realm, it is who we are when we are at our best. It is what is possible when we give ourselves completely to a cause. It is what we are capable of when we are trained, disciplined, and focused over an extended period of time.

In ministry, it is what is possible when people are fervently praying, leaders are going above and beyond the call of duty, and spiritual priorities have greater weight than personal privacy and leisure.

On a spiritual level, the first step in this battle comes in realizing that there are two worlds that exist. There is the *physical* world, which is what we can see, touch, feel, experience, and measure. There is also a *spiritual* world that is not as easy to see, touch, feel, experience, and measure—unless you know what to look for.

True next-level living means placing as much focus and effort on addressing what is happening in the spirit realm as you do in the physical realm. In fact, more is needed.

Authentic next-level living requires constant, extraordinary effort, self-discipline, selflessness, being teachable, and the ability to see and live life, and all its experiences, through the eyes of Christ. These are the hallmarks of next-level achievements.

Next-level living is not something that can be accomplished by an event, a trip, a conference, or even an incredible moment of revelation. Just like the illustrations above, this can only happen as the result of extraordinary effort, self-discipline, and going above and beyond the call of duty *over an extended period of time*. Most of us can commit to the moments, the trips, and the events, but it's in the long haul that we are losing the battle. Yes, there will be sacrifice, and, yes, it will demand a major overhaul of priorities, but I believe with all my heart that the victory that lies at the finish line will be worth every moment spent and every sacrifice made.

That, in a nutshell, is what this book is designed to do. It is designed to help you see what is true about the world we live in and enable you to live and serve with discernment, wisdom, and courage. Like the lights of the city, the world has a thousand messages it wants us to hear, a million voices vying for our attention, and hundreds of philosophies on how to best live for God. My goal is to help you see beneath the surface; hear that still, small voice amidst the deafening cry of the world; and take courageous steps of faith.

In short, we cannot simply go through the motions. We must understand that there is a war raging all around. It is a war you signed up for when you declared yourself a Christian and a war that only intensified the day you took on one of the most treasured titles given by God—His disciple.

But this is a war that Scripture tells us is for the winning, and it is not a war we wage alone, for He has promised that He will go with us into battle and that He will defend us, protect us, and deliver us at every turn.

> And he will turn many of the children of Israel to the Lord their God. He will also go before Him in the spirit and power of Elijah, "to turn the hearts of the fathers to the children," and the disobedient *to the wisdom of the just, to make ready a people prepared for the Lord.*
> —Luke 1:16–17, emphasis added

That is my purpose, my aim, my call—and the reason for this book.

SECTION I

DRAW NEAR

But now in Christ Jesus you who once were far off have been brought near by the blood of Christ. For He Himself is our peace, who has made both one, and has broken *down the middle wall of separation*.
—Ephesians 2:13–14, emphasis added

chapter 1

THE PLAY IS OVER

For look, the wicked bend their bows;
>they set their arrows against the strings
to shoot from the shadows
>at the upright in heart.
When the foundations are being destroyed,
>*what can the righteous do?*
The LORD is in his holy temple;
>the LORD is on his heavenly throne.
He observes the sons of men;
>his eyes examine them.
>—Psalm 11:2–4, NIV, emphasis added

I WANT TO OPEN THIS CHAPTER WITH A REALITY CHECK. ALTHOUGH what follows is a fictitious story, it carries some alarming truths about the enemy's plan of attack against us. We need to wake up!

Satan called a worldwide convention of demons. In his opening address he said, "We can't keep Christians from going to church. We can't keep them from reading their Bibles and knowing the truth. We can't even keep them from forming an intimate relationship with their Savior. Once they gain that connection with Jesus, our power over them is broken. So let them go to their churches, and let them sing their songs, but steal their time so they don't have time to develop a relationship with Jesus Christ. Distract them from gaining hold of their Savior and maintaining that vital connection throughout their day!"

"How shall we do this?" his demons shouted. "Keep them busy in the nonessentials of life, and invent innumerable schemes to occupy their minds," he answered. "Tempt them to spend, spend, spend, and borrow, borrow, borrow. Persuade the wives to go to work for long hours and the husbands to work six or seven days each week, ten to twelve hours a day, so they can afford their lavish lifestyles. Keep them from spending time with their children. As their families fragment, their homes will offer no escape from the pressures of work!

"Keep skinny, beautiful models in magazines and on television so husbands will believe that outward beauty is what's important, and soon they'll become dissatisfied with their wives. Keep the wives too tired to love their husbands at night. Give them headaches too! If they don't give their husbands the love they need, their husbands will begin to look elsewhere. That will fragment their families quickly! It will work!" said Satan.

It was quite a plan! The demons went eagerly to their assignments, causing Christians everywhere to get busier and more rushed, going here and there, having little time for their God or their families. Meanwhile, the army of Satan began to march and take ground. It went into our schools, teaching science without a creator; into our homes, imprisoning minds with the click of a computer mouse; and into the public square, demanding total allegiance to their false gods and acceptance of their immoral lifestyles.

"It can work!" cried Satan as the demons cheered with glee. "When do we start?" the demons asked. Satan smiled, nodded with confidence, and said, "Look all around you. We're already here."

—Author Unknown

A History of Surprises

"The voice of one crying in the wilderness: 'Prepare the way of the LORD'" (Matt. 3:3). With that incredibly prophetic announcement, the stage was set. The forerunner, John the Baptist, with that single message set a series of historical circumstances into motion that would change the face of religion forever. Jesus was here, and as a result, nothing would ever be the same. A revolution had begun, and the promised Savior had arrived. What ensued was a revolution that would not only change the world but also pave the way of salvation for any and all who would call upon His name until He comes again.

Fast-forward: The year is 1776, and behold, a second forerunner has emerged, another voice crying out in the wilderness. This voice is declaring an altogether different message. Paul Revere rides on his horse from town to town, declaring, "The British are coming! The British are coming!" And with that one call to arms, a revolution of an entirely different kind began—one that would change the course of world history for centuries to come. What ensued was a fight for religious freedom for any and all who would declare independence from the tyrannical, religiously intolerant regime called the British Empire.

Fast-forward again: The time is the first decade of the twenty-first century, and the voice we hear is the Word of God. The signs of the times are crying out to a deafened, desensitized church, shouting, "Wake up! The enemy is coming." Satan and his army are on our shores, invading like an army of locusts while we go about acting as if all is well, seeing only the mirror on our wall and never even taking a glance into the kingdom to see what is really going on above the ground in the heavenlies and in the high places.

> And as it was in the days of Noah, so it will be also in the days of the Son of Man: They ate, they drank, they married wives, they were given in marriage, until the day that Noah entered the ark, and the flood came and destroyed them all. Likewise as it was also in the days of Lot: They ate, they drank, they bought, they sold, they planted, they built; but on the day that Lot went out of Sodom it rained fire and brimstone from heaven and destroyed them all. Even so will it be in the day when the Son of Man is revealed.
>
> —Luke 17:26–30

THE PLAY IS OVER

The great British author and playwright David Lodge was sitting in the audience one crisp, cool autumn day, watching and enjoying the very play he had written some time before. He, like the hundreds of who had come to see the play that day, sat mesmerized, immersed in an entirely different reality for those brief few hours as the events of the stage played out before them. For a few hours in time, the cares of the world and the comings and goings of everything outside the theater walls seemed as distant as a foreign country as they were swept up into an entirely different reality while never leaving their seats.

Then, something extraordinary happened. During the course of the play, there came a scene where one of the actors crossed the stage to turn on a radio. To the actor and to the audience, it was not some dramatic part of the play—just something to occupy the actor's actions while the dialogue continued—but as he turned on that radio and turned the knob to find a station, suddenly there came a voice across the airwaves announcing the death of President John F. Kennedy. A bit startled, the actor, while never breaking character, simply hustled back over to the radio and turned it down, but it was too late.

One by one, different members of the audience began to slip out of the auditorium to go make a phone call, and soon the buzz swept the theater. John F. Kennedy, the leader of the free world, had been assassinated. Suddenly, the play was over. Reality had rushed in across those airwaves that day, and with that one profound announcement, nothing would ever be the same. Life as we knew it would change dramatically over the next days and weeks as families huddled around television sets and radios, grasping for every piece of information they could find. Sporting events were canceled, businesses did not do business as usual, and the churches were filled beyond capacity as a nation mourned their fallen leader and seethed at the evil that fell him.

With a different set of characters and location, the same story occurred many years back in 1941. That fateful December morning, the Japanese air force came whistling though the harbor completely unprovoked and bombed a sleeping, unsuspecting navy who had let their guard down for a brief moment in time. They too were thinking all was well, believing they were hundreds of thousands of miles from danger. Though the very thing they had prepared for was the eventuality of having to defend their great nation, their focus was not on war and the possible attack of an enemy but rather on the routine of the day, a big party the night before, and the comings and goings of their everyday lives on the ship and in their homes on the shore.

For a brief moment in time, the greatest military on the face of the earth let its guard down, and the enemy crept in, leaving death and destruction in its wake. In that instant, we became a nation at war, but only after inevitable loss of life.

Once again, life as we knew it changed dramatically. We all huddled around radios, grasping for every piece of information we could find. Sporting events were canceled, businesses did not do business as usual, and the churches were filled beyond capacity.

Fast-forward one last time to September 11, 2001. Same story, same nation, different set of characters and location, but the same deadly results. Once again, the most powerful nation on the planet, while thinking themselves untouchable by the radical elements of the world, slumbered as we went about our daily affairs, leaving peace, security, and the protection of our way of life to the generals, the government, and the police forces trained to protect us, only to discover the enemy had been among us for years. The evil that showed itself that fateful September morning had fooled us by simply blending in. They knew one thing for certain about us, the enemy they intended to destroy: we could not see their invasion on the horizon because our eyes were fixed on ourselves.

They knew our weak spot. They knew that by and large, we were not a people concerned with the affairs of the world, not a people who had been on the lookout for an enemy, and not a nation preparing for war. They knew we were just like the audience watching the play that fateful day. They knew that our pursuit of affluence and leisure and our focus on pursuing the American Dream would blind us to the very things that would ultimately destroy thousands of us in an instant.

Thousands died. Our nation once again turned its eyes toward God as Republicans and Democrats alike stood side by side, singing "God Bless America." Once again, life as we knew it changed dramatically. We all huddled around television sets and radios, grasping for every piece of information we could find. Sporting events were canceled, businesses did not do business as usual, and the churches were filled beyond capacity. Within weeks, we were all looking for someone to blame. Republicans went back to being Republicans, and Democrats went back to being Democrats. People eventually resumed their daily routines, and the American mind-set once again resumed its preoccupation with "me and mine" as the "play" resumed and the characters on the stage picked up where they left off.

Today, the church finds itself as vulnerable to attack as it has ever been, not because of weak churches and false doctrine, but because of the focus of its millions of rank-and-file members. The stage has been set. The signs are everywhere, but millions of evangelical Christians—at least in the United States—are no different from those thousands of unsuspecting sailors at Pearl Harbor. They are just as vulnerable as those thousands of innocent men and women working in the highest quarters of the World Trade Center. They are just as under attack as those brave men and women in the late 1700s who fought the great Revolutionary War. They were just going about their daily affairs as usual, unaware that an enemy army had landed on their shores, hell-bent on destroying any and all who would dare declare allegiance to anyone other than the king of England.

The common factor in all of these sneak attacks was an enemy who had crept in with the intent of killing and destroying not just innocent men and women, but also our way of life, our belief systems, and our freedom to worship our God. We must wake up immediately and make haste. We must realize that the play is over. Millions of souls hang in the balance, as "multitudes, multitudes in the valley of decision" (Joel 3:14). The enemy seeks to have us as his own, taking not just our way of life but our souls as well. The only difference this time around is that it is not someone else's children who are at stake. It is not a battle to be fought in someone else's cities and lands. It is here, right here among us now, and the prize is the next generation. The enemy, Satan, will stop at nothing to have them for his own.

> I am concerned for the security of our great Nation; not so much because of any threat from without, but because of the insidious forces working from within.[1]
>
> —Douglas MacArthur

Same problem, different day, infinitely multiplied. Wake up, mighty church of God, followers of Jesus! There is a war that is raging, and the prize the enemy seeks is simple yet profound. The enemy demands surrender and has no regard for human life. What's at stake? Simply put, the mind of man and the children of man. Wake up, draw near, and fall in. The battle is nearer than you think, and the enemy closer than you have imagined.

chapter 2

CONSECRATION: THE PROVEN PATH TO A NEXT-LEVEL RELATIONSHIP

> Then you will call upon Me and go and pray to Me, and I will listen to you. And you will seek Me and find Me, when you search for Me with all your heart. I will be found by you, says the LORD, and I will bring you back from your captivity.
>
> —Jeremiah 29:12–14

GEORGE WASHINGTON, ABRAHAM LINCOLN, BILL BRIGHT, JAMES Dobson, Billy Graham, Chuck Smith, Beth Moore, Joyce Meyer, Jerry Falwell, Mark Rutland, John MacArthur, Jack Hyles, Paul Chapel, and a score of other great men and women of the faith have engineered some of the greatest moves of God in the history of the church, resulting in millions of souls finding salvation in Christ. At the root of every great move of God throughout history there has been a handful of people who set themselves apart, went before their God for hours at a time, and simply cried out to their Lord and Savior for a supernatural touch. These people include Charles Spurgeon, Martin Luther, Dwight L. Moody, Abraham, Moses, David, Peter, Paul, and the list goes on and on. All experienced an anointing directly from the throne and were filled with the power of the Holy Spirit.

GOD'S ANOINTING ON ORDINARY PEOPLE

How does a regular guy or gal with a full-time job, a family, and an event calendar filled with activity and responsibility carve out a spiritual life that even remotely resembles the lives described above? Well, I would imagine the same kinds of questions had to be running through the mind of Peter,

Paul, and anyone else who "got all the way in" throughout history. But what you must understand is that God has been in the business of using ordinary people to accomplish His extraordinary work on Earth for centuries. So what I'm talking about, as it relates to you, is not dropping everything on your plate and moving in with monks. What I am asking you to do over the next three or four weeks is to simply go the extra mile, thirty to forty-five minutes a day, for a short season of your life to see what God might be saying to you about you and your role in His great plan.

Let's take a look at a very special word: *consecration.* Look at the definitions offered below, and try to pick which one most resembles your purpose for the time you are spending working through this book.

- Irrevocable devotion to the worship of God
- Devotion to a purpose with deep solemnity or dedication
- Dedication to a sacred purpose
- Dedication to the service of God of one's person or possessions

Did any of these strike a cord with you? Simply put, the process you find yourself involved in is a process whereby you are committing to *set yourself apart* for a season to grow closer to Christ and to the person He intends for you to be. Now you may be asking yourself, "What does this have to do with all of the 'going-to-war' stuff from the last chapter?" The first step in the battle plan is to begin to *draw near* to the God of the universe so that He can begin to do a work in you, just you, to fit you for battle and to prepare you for all He has for you to do.

> For though we walk in the flesh, we do not war according to the flesh. For the weapons of our warfare are not carnal but mighty in God for pulling down strongholds, casting down arguments and every high thing that exalts itself against the knowledge of God, bringing every thought into captivity to the obedience of Christ.
> —2 Corinthians 10:3–5

Make no mistake, there is a mission specifically for you, but to send you out as you are would be like sending a sheep to the slaughter. There is work to do to get you ready, and you must first commit to that. Thus the need for consecration, setting yourself apart, carving out that thirty to forty-five minutes per day in order to take the journey from where you are to where He is.

KNOWING GOD

The path to your purpose leads through the narrow way of relationship with Christ. Now, that sounds simple enough, but you would be amazed at everything people do to try to get around having a relationship with God. We try serving in every ministry possible, attending every special service we can find, in search of that special word from God just for us. We even try through experiences—incredible experiences such as powerful worship services, missions trips, and witnessing—to avoid doing the hard work of relationship with Christ. Why do we do that?

We are such a task-oriented, score-keeping people, but I am here to tell you that God does not keep score the way we do. The Book of Matthew says it like this:

> Not everyone who says to Me, "Lord, Lord," shall enter the kingdom of heaven, but he who does the will of My Father in heaven. Many will say to Me in that day, "Lord, Lord, have we not prophesied in Your name, cast out demons in Your name, and done many wonders in Your name?" And then I will declare to them, "*I never knew you.*"
> —Matthew 7:21–23, emphasis added

"I never knew you." Wow! Those are powerful words. Do you know Him, or do you just know about Him? It can be so easy to make our Christianity all about ourselves and avoid relationship altogether with tragic consequences on both sides of the grave. My favorite actor is Kurt Russell. I think he's awesome, and I love his movies. Now, I can read all about Kurt, think about Kurt, do stuff for Kurt, tell people about Kurt, and even contribute to Kurt's favorite charities. I can even refer to him as "Kurt" all through this paragraph, but should I ever want to visit Kurt at his home, when his security people tell him Rich Rogers is here to see him, his response will be,

"I don't know him. I never knew him. Send him away." I am no more than a groupie or a fan, really. Some might even classify me as a stalker if I am not careful.

We have too many Christian stalkers. They run to every religious experience they can find. They sign up for every activity, attend every service, stand in every greeting line to shake hands with the pastor, and even tell their friends they know famous pastors, but none of those things equal relationship.

While it is not an easy thing to know famous people or even famous pastors anymore, it is entirely possible to really *know* God. In fact, there is nothing He desires more. It is the very reason He created you—for relationship.

MOVING TO THE NEXT LEVEL

Now, here is a challenge I am going to pose to you. As you journey through this book, I am going to challenge you to read and process no more than one chapter per day. The first chapter was written to help you see the importance of getting all the way in and living life at the next level. In this chapter, I have challenged you to a consecration of your life and time that will lead you into a relationship with God that is better than anything you have experienced before. Now, I am asking you to commit to the process of growth and to resist the urge to simply finish this book. If you will read each day's chapter, underline, put your comments in the margins, and then spend time reflecting and praying about what we talked about that day, I guarantee you will experience growth and revelation and specific direction for your life, not just from me, but from the Holy Spirit through your time immersed in the process.

chapter 3

DRAWING NEAR IN SEVEN EASY STEPS

My sheep hear My voice, and I know them, and they follow Me. And I give them eternal life, and they shall never perish; neither shall anyone snatch them out of My hand.
—John 10:27–28, emphasis added

Therefore, brothers, since we have confidence to enter the Most Holy Place by the blood of Jesus, by a new and living way opened for us through the curtain, that is, his body, and since we have a great priest over the house of God, *let us draw near to God with a sincere heart in full assurance of* faith...having our bodies washed with pure water. Let us hold unswervingly to the hope we profess, for he who promised is faithful.
—Hebrews 10:19–23, NIV, emphasis added

AS WE MOVE TO THE NEXT STEP OF DRAWING NEAR, LET US remember that there are two worlds that exist—the physical world that we can see, touch, feel, experience, and measure; and the spiritual world that is not so easy to see, touch, feel, experience, and measure. Understanding and knowing the reality of these worlds is the first step in learning to walk and live a life at the next level. We can know that both are equally as real, but where we really miss it is in the vast amount of attention we give to the physical world and how little consideration we give to the spirit world.

TWO WORLDS, ONE MIND

The concept that this book is named for, next level, refers simply to the fact that there are two worlds, and the spirit world is what I refer to in this book as the next level. Do you believe this? Do you believe that there really are evil forces, a devil, demons, angels, and an unseen world? I absolutely do. In fact, I believe that all we encounter here in our earthly existence is engineered by forces that are at work all around us. The Book of Ephesians says it like this:

> Finally, my brethren, be strong in the Lord and in the power of His might. Put on the whole armor of God, that you may be able to stand against the wiles of the devil. For we do not wrestle against flesh and blood, but against principalities, against powers, against the rulers of darkness of this age, against spiritual hosts of wickedness in the heavenly places. Therefore take up the whole armor of God, that you may be able to withstand in the evil day, and having done all, to stand.
> —Ephesians 6:10–13

In order to truly live at the next level, you must begin to focus on and address what is happening in the spiritual world as much as you do in the physical world. This needs to be an extraordinary focus and effort given over an extended period of time. You must have the discipline, selflessness, and teachability to be able to see all of life's experiences through the eyes of Christ.

Now, that being established, you must understand that to see what is happening in the spirit realm, you must begin to develop your spiritual eyes, ears, and heart. How? By drawing near, beginning today. How does one draw near? you ask. By walking down a very narrow road—one step at a time, one day at a time—for this season of your life.

DRAWING NEAR IN SEVEN EASY STEPS

I am about to give you a process that, if you commit to it, will revolutionize your faith and bring you to the very foot of the throne of God. It is not some mystical, magical formula, but rather a simple, weekly plan of action that will take you deeper than you have ever been as long as you commit and get all the way in. I call these seven simple steps the seven disciplines of the faith.

1. Prayer time and prayer place
2. Bible study
3. Church attendance
4. Giving
5. Serving
6. Worship
7. Connecting with other believers

Now, I know what many of you are thinking. Some are thinking, "This sounds too simple." Others are saying, "Hey, this sounds like a religion of works." And still others are saying, "How can one person do all of these things?" Well, allow me to chime in here and tell you a few things about committing to the disciplines of the faith. First, it is easy in some ways, and in other ways it's not. It's easily understood but harder to do. It takes work, time, commitment, and discipline. Second, yes, it is "works" absolutely, but what relationship doesn't take work? A marriage will not last without doing the hard work of relating, living together, finding common ground, encouraging, helping, talking, and... (pick your verb).

Relationships take work, and that is what this is all about. The secret to growing in Christ is the same as the secret to finding your destiny, your purpose, and your mission in life. The secret? Simply put, the path to everything God has for you can only be found through a deep, committed, loving, and relating relationship with Christ. How? Let's look at the seven disciplines of the faith.

1. Prayer time and prayer place: Spend time in conversation with Him—talking, listening, interceding, praising, worshiping, listening some more—communicating. This is the kind of communication you can only have when you stop what you are doing, get alone, and look into His eyes, giving intentional, focused, personal attention.

2. Bible study: You can't possibly hear the voice of God if you never allow Him to open His mouth and speak to you. The Bible is simply what God has to say to you, about you, and about Himself and His ways. Reading this book can serve as your time in the Word, as there will be passages of Scripture woven throughout, but I would also encourage those of you who are up for a challenge to read Psalms during this time as well.

3. Church attendance: This is a tough one for some, but I have to challenge you to get under a great Bible teacher, pastor, and ministry. Why is it so many of us love God but cannot stand being with His people? What, pray tell, do you think heaven will be like? A bunch of individual cities for one? Also, church hopping doesn't count. Get in a church, even if just for this month, and commit to attending faithfully.

4. Giving: This is a *really* tough one for some of you, and for now, I am not going to put any kind of requirements on your giving. If you know you are to tithe and you are doing that, then that is what you need to do, and you know why, but for the rest of you, I want to challenge you to give something, and something substantial while you read through this book. Maybe you are not ready for 10 percent right now. The Lord loves it when people give cheerfully from their heart; He is not moved by a begrudging tenth, so start where you can and let's see what happens.

5. Serving: The church is simply God's people. In that mix, though, are a number of needs that require ministries within the church to supply. These ministries are made up of people—flesh-and-blood people just like you and me. I want to challenge you to spend a month or two volunteering in a ministry. Now, don't hold out for the perfect ministry.

Just jump in and volunteer to help wherever help is needed. No strings attached. Then watch and see what the Lord teaches you about Himself and about you over the course of the next few weeks.

6. Worship: While there are many different ways to "worship" God, such as giving and service, what I am after here is something directly linked to the number-one discipline of the faith—your prayer time and your prayer place. How does one do that, you might ask. Well, if you are a bit new to this, I have a prayer method for worship I would like to suggest. It is easy to remember and covers many of the basics for worship, which is a steady, focused time with the Lord, exalting Him for all He is, has, and will do. It is easy to follow. It is the acronym ACTS. Simply get alone with the Lord, and walk through these simple steps:

A—Adoration: Just spend a few moments in adoration, recognizing Him for who He is—His awesomeness, His power, His truth, His mighty works, His creation, His love for us, His sacrifices on the cross, just the very fact that He is God—*your* God. You may find that a few moments turn into a much longer period of time than you expected.

C—Confession: This simply means confessing your sins to God. Scripture says that if we will just confess our sins to Him, He is faithful to forgive us our sins. Just be honest. Tell Him where you have blown it, and then ask Him for His forgiveness. Ask Him to reveal to you sin that you have yet to confess or maybe even things you have done that you have justified in your mind but are sin before the Lord. Ask Him to reveal those things as well. He *will* forgive. Then repent by committing to turning from that sinful practice. Remember His blood that was shed on the cross for you, and know that your sins are not just forgiven, they are also blotted out.

T—Thanksgiving: He loves to hear us remember the things He has done for us. God loves grateful children, just like you with your own children. It is so important that we develop an attitude of gratitude. Gratitude improves our attitude and our entire perspective on everything. Be a grateful and expressive person.

S—Supplication: This is the part where you make your needs and your requests known to Him through your spoken word. Be honest. Tell Him your desires, your needs, the people you are praying for, and everything you desire to know or to see happen.

This acronym, ACTS, is an excellent way to pray whether you have been a Christian for twenty years or two weeks. It hits all the bases, and if done with a sincere heart, it can result in a powerful time of prayer, worship, and intimacy with Christ.

Now, last but not least, number seven—connecting.

7. Connecting with other believers: This is probably the hardest discipline for people to commit to, especially men, but it is also the most necessary. It is critical that you connect to other believers in meaningful, personal, intentional relationship. There are many ways to do this, but one of the best ways is to commit to becoming involved in a small group at your church. What is most important is that you tell the Lord that you will do this if He will show you how and with whom.

Remember, the goal is not simply to have "stuff to do." The purpose for this, first and foremost, is to begin your journey and to commit to a process. You must realize that growth, destiny, purpose, and preparation for all God has for you comes only through the narrow way of relationship with Christ over an extended period of time.

For the eyes of the LORD run to and fro throughout the whole earth, to show Himself strong on behalf of those whose heart is loyal to Him.

—2 Chronicles 16:9

Show me your ways, O LORD,
　　teach me your paths;
guide me in your truth and teach me,
　　for you are God my Savior,
　　and my hope is in you all day long…

Who, then, is the man that fears the LORD?
　　He will instruct him in the way chosen for him.
He will spend his days in prosperity,
　　and his descendents will inherit the land.
The LORD confides in those who fear him;
　　he makes his covenant known to them.

—Psalm 25:4–5, 12–14, NIV, emphasis added

Wow! What an incredible promise. God will instruct you in the way chosen for you. What a powerful thing for the Lord to confide in you. Jeremiah says it even stronger:

For I know the thoughts that I think toward you, says the LORD, thoughts of peace and not of evil, to give you a future and a hope. Then you will call upon Me and go and pray to Me, and I will listen to you. *And you will seek Me and find Me, when you search for Me with all your heart.* I will be found by you, says the LORD, and I will bring you back from your captivity.

—Jeremiah 29:11–14, emphasis added

Don't you want to know Him like that? Don't you? I do! Well, I want to close this chapter with one more quick next-level principle.

YOU ARE AS CLOSE TO JESUS AS YOU WANT TO BE

You are in the driver's seat on this one. I have given you the formula. I have explained each step in detail. Now it is you that must choose how you will spend your day. It is you that will decide just how close you get to your destiny, your purpose, your mission on Earth. Will there be distractions? Yes. Will the stuff of life come up and interrupt? Absolutely.

This is why I close with two simple questions. One, if Satan wanted to keep you from drawing near to God, how would he do it? Two, if Satan wanted to keep you from doing the seven disciplines of the faith, how would he accomplish that? Think about those two simple questions for a minute, and then remember your answer the next time you feel tempted to skip a few days. Time is too precious and the need too great. You are needed in the battle, and it is imperative that you complete your training and enter the fray, for the laborers are few for the "multitudes, multitudes in the valley of decision."

That's enough for today. We'll pick up from here in the next chapter, but for now, I just want to challenge you to realize that all of heaven has taken notice of this bold step you are taking—this season of being set apart. I know for a fact that you have a Savior who eagerly waits to meet with you each day during this journey. Some time today, before you go to bed, find a prayer place where you won't be interrupted, and lift up your voice and give your love to Him. Ask Him your questions, commit to a process, and allow Him to do with you what He wants to do. Big beginnings for some, profound for others, necessary for all.

chapter 4

CONNECTING WITH OTHER BELIEVERS

There are dimensions of our glorious King that will never be revealed to the casual, disinterested worshiper. There are walls of intercession that will never be scaled by dispassionate religious service. But when you take steps to break out of the ordinary and worship Him as He deserves, you will begin to see facets of His being you never knew existed. He will begin to share secrets with you about Himself, His plans, His desires for you. When you worship God as He deserves, He is magnified.[1]

—Jentezen Franklin

THE TALE I AM ABOUT TO TELL IS ABOUT THREE SITUATIONS: TWO of which are families, and the third is an individual. All three stories are true; however, the names have been changed. One has a very happy ending, and two have very sad, tragic endings, but all three illustrate the same point. Contrary to the song made popular by the Beatles, "All You Need Is Love," love is *not* all you need. Not if you are going to be everything He designed you to be. As you read each true story, I challenge you to look deep into your own life and see if there is a message for you found in the lives of one of these families and individuals.

A TALE OF THREE FAMILIES

The players

Couple #1—Bob and Emily: If you saw Bob and Emily ten years ago, you would have seen the picture of success. Bob had a six-figure income. Both of them were very attractive physically, and they were very involved in their church.

Bob even led worship as a volunteer, and Emily was one of the worship singers. Bob was one of the founding members of this new church and as such was considered the "on-staff" worship pastor, although he refused to accept any pay. Bob and Emily drove very nice cars; had lots of friends and lots of things, including a boat and a vacation house in the mountains; and were very happy together. All was well for this happy couple, and after a few years of marriage, the Lord blessed them with a beautiful baby boy.

Couple #2—Sam and Julie: Sam and Julie were a lot like Bob and Emily. Sam, as a single man, was very athletic and enjoyed water sports and basketball nights at the church, but after watching all of his friends marry off one by one, he too got the itch. When Julie visited the church one summer as a summer missionary, he made his move, and a year later, the two were married. Sam made very good money, while Julie finished her degree program to become a teacher.

Sam and Julie became very good friends with Bob and Emily as they began attending the same church. They did many things together and spent a great deal of time at each other's houses as well. For all four, life was good!

Single dad—John: John was a college professor and a single dad. His son, Rudy, was only five years old and a product of John's second failed marriage. He had two daughters in their midtwenties who were grown and gone. John was in his late forties when we first met him. As is the case with many of today's college professors, John was very liberal politically, a bit cynical religiously, and was not short on opinions about churches, God, or Christians, but he was our friend. We never focused too much on our differences, and instead tried to love him and be good neighbors.

John was a good neighbor as well and a very good dad. John had his son, Rudy, only every other weekend, and it was not hard to look beneath the scholarly surface and see the pain and the sadness he felt when those weekends would come to an end. He constantly worried about Rudy, but there really was not much he could do. Even though he could provide his son a much better life, and even though the life Rudy went home to when he left John was precarious and unstable, it was out of John's ability to control. The courts had spoken. Worse yet, John did not lose it all because of anything he did or wished. His wife had just chosen to leave him for another man, and there was nothing he could do. John did not hold out much hope for Rudy, and we believed at the time that John dealt with bouts of depression as a result of all this.

THE SECOND HALF OF THE STORY

Three situations; three sets of circumstances; with three different results.

Now let me explain the next five or six years in the lives of each to show you how things turned out. Any guesses? Two couples seem to have it all. They were living the American Dream, while the third scenario seemed to be almost hopeless. Whom will God bless? How will these lives turn out? I encourage you to see if you see yourself or your life circumstances in any of these scenarios. See if there is a message for you somewhere in these real-life situations. Let's see about the rest of the story.

Couple #1—Bob and Emily

One summer, Bob, Emily, and their one-year-old son went on a month-long vacation together. Upon returning home, Bob was given some rather abrupt news. When Bob showed up for the church staff meeting, there was another fellow at the table. It was the new worship pastor. The senior pastor had decided to replace Bob, who had always served as a volunteer, with a new paid staff person the pastor felt would do a better job. You see, the senior pastor had tried to convince Bob on many occasions to play certain songs and to keep the tempo upbeat and positive, but Bob loved the slow songs, the ones with emotion. So when the interim guy came along with just the right songs, just the right tempo, and possibly just the right servant's heart, Bob was out—rightly or wrongly.

The pastor did his best to try to let Bob down as easy as he could, but the damage had been done and the hurt was deep, despite the good face Bob tried to put on.

That would be a pretty hard thing for anyone to handle, but this story is really all about the seven years after this event. For the next seven years, Bob and his small family (soon to be four) visited just about every evangelical church in the area. They had a blast. They never had to spend time preparing anything or working in child care. They even got the best parking spaces available.

When there was a famous speaker at one church, they got to hear him in person. When there was a special music group at another church, they were there. If they got up too late, they just went to the megachurch right down the street. If they got up early, they could attend their favorite church at the north end of the county. They had the best of every world, were thoroughly entertained, and got to shake hands with every big-name Christian personality you could think of.

So how on earth do you explain that after five years of this fantastic life with three beautiful children, a loving wife, and a dog, Bob and Emily were divorced? Bob now suffers from deep bouts of depression and has been left wondering what he will do with the rest of his life. Bob now only gets to see his children on specified days and holidays, and even then, the mutually agreed-upon supervisor is never out of earshot. Emily has three children she will now raise on her own, with all of the financial pains that accompany the life of a single mom.

Why? How could this happen? They had it all: a six-figure income, a beautiful home, a boat, and all the while singing praise and worship or listening to the greatest preachers in the country week in and week out—in person. How? Why?

Couple #2—Sam and Julie

Sam and Julie's situation is very similar to Bob and Emily's. In fact, as I mentioned before, they all went to the same church, the one where Bob had been replaced. Sam and Julie were very happy. They attended church every week. Julie was a deaf interpreter, and Sam was a faithful layman.

Then, a pretty significant event happened in Sam's and Julie's lives. The senior pastor of this church of about three hundred came to Sam and asked him to consider being a deacon. While this was quite an honor, it was a scary proposition for Sam, one he was not quite sure he was up for. One thing led to another, and for some reason one Sunday, they decided to attend the large megachurch across town with a few of their friends.

Sam and Julie loved the service. The music was incredible, the message was top quality, and they felt warm fuzzies all throughout the service. It was a very different experience than the smaller church experience they were accustomed to, and Sam, being a private person anyway, really liked the anonymity he was afforded in a megachurch congregation.

Over the next few months, Sam and Julie went from frequent visitors to regular attendees at this church. Before you know it, they became members. They rarely missed a Sunday service. It wasn't long until they had a little girl, and over the next three or four years, they were faithful attendees of this wonderful megachurch.

Sounds great, right? Sadly, their fate became the same as Bob and Emily's, and not long after Sam and Julie separated, they were divorced. Where could this plan have possibly gone wrong? They weren't church hopping; they were regular attendees. They lifted their hands during worship, and many weeks they were moved very deeply by the music or the message. They loved coming to church and always left feeling renewed and inspired. So what could have possibly gone wrong?

Bob and Emily, Sam and Julie—they had it all. What went wrong? Simply put, they suffered from one of the most fatal spiritual diseases known to the church—and for that matter, marriages. They suffered severely from the heart killer called disconnect. This was coupled with the second most deadly disease known to relationships and belief systems—they never developed roots, so the plant above the ground could not survive. It was basic science.

Both couples rarely missed church, but they never got all the way in, either. Even Sam and Julie, although attending every Sunday morning, attended in anonymity, as did Bob and Emily. They would slip in and slip out, never developing relationships. They never interacted with others. They were never in an environment where they even had to open their Bible; the verses were on the screen. They never grew deeper, and as a result, when the storms came, they could not survive.

Ephesians chapter 4 holds an incredible passage of pure truth related to this topic. It says:

It was he who gave some to be apostles, some to be prophets, some to be evangelists, and some to be pastors and teachers, to prepare God's people for works of service, *so that the body of Christ may be built up* until we all reach unity in the faith and *in the knowledge of the Son of God and become mature, attaining to the whole measure of the fullness of Christ.*

Then we will no longer be infants, tossed back and forth by the waves, and blown here and there by every wind of teaching and by the cunning and craftiness of men in their deceitful scheming. Instead, speaking the truth in love, *we will in all things grow up into him who is the Head, that is, Christ.* From him the whole body, joined and *held together by every supporting ligament,* grows and builds itself up in love, as each part does its work.

—Ephesians 4:11–16, NIV, emphasis added

To emphasize the power and the truth of this passage, one Sunday morning recently my pastor gave a visual illustration of what this passage means and the implications it has for today's Christian. He placed a shoebox-sized box on top of the pulpit and explained that for a believer to simply attend church weekly, while separating himself or herself from the rest of the body in lifestyle and geography, would be like taking your hand and severing it from your arm and placing it in a box. Now, the body would heal, find a way to manage without the hand, and then continue to grow and mature into adulthood. Meanwhile, the severed hand would not continue to grow, would not be useful to the rest of the body, and would live the rest of its existence in an isolated, lifeless state of decay. That's powerful stuff, especially as it relates to the stories you just read.

Please do not miss what I am saying here. The only way you will ever develop, grow, and mature in your faith is through relationship with other believers (fellowship), through studying God's Word (discipleship), and through committing your time and resources to God (service). You must do one of the most difficult tasks for many people, especially men. You must connect. You must grow deeper. You must mature. Otherwise you are building your house on sand, quicksand even. It won't last. It will not stand the test of time, and it will not bring you closer to your Savior, no matter how many tears you shed during a worship service.

Sunday mornings, and this is especially true for larger churches, if not taken with a steady diet of fellowship, relationship, and accountability, will accomplish little more than a constant diet of candy bars and chocolate. It will not sustain life.

What's the point? The point is that without getting all the way "in," your experience will still leave you feeling empty. In a later chapter, I am going to ask you to get on your knees before your God and to declare your intentions. No matter how powerful that moment may be, and I believe it will be a defining moment, you must be willing to get all the way in with your God, be willing to draw near to Him, and be willing to let Him connect you to His body through His Word, service to Him, and fellowship with other believers.

> People need more than bread for their life; they must feed on every word of God.
>
> —Matthew 4:4, author's paraphrase

Now, let me finish with the last story. Same principle; different players; different results.

Single dad—John

A very interesting thing happened one Sunday. John showed up at our church. We had never pushed our church on John, never really invited him officially, but week after week, my wife would weave stories into her conversations with John that involved our church. All of a sudden, there he was. He didn't even sit with us, but he was there.

Soon, he was attending pretty much every Sunday, and the weekends that his son, Rudy, was with him, he would bring him. Interestingly enough, John was a very protective father and therefore would volunteer to help out in his son's Sunday school class every time he was with him. We would see him during the week, and he would talk about something he liked about the service but never about any kind of major life change or belief system overhaul.

Then, slowly, day by day, week by week, we began to see a change in John as the Lord began to get ahold of him and touch him, heal him, and draw him unto Himself. After about a year, John was a regular attendee, and we could see a changed heart and a changed life. There were major court custody dates on the horizon, and for the first time, John had to put his Savior to the test.

To make a long and wonderful story short, now seven years later, John never misses a Sunday, has full custody of his son, has a fiancée, and is notice-ably, physically, and in his countenance a changed man. He turned to Christ in his greatest hour of need, and Christ met him right there and changed his life. John humbled himself and each week became more and more involved in the Sunday school program, men's ministry, and other ministries as he began to mature.

John never would have made it if all he had done was come every Sunday morning, listen for an hour, and then go home. He needed something real. He needed something he could touch and feel and take hold of. So, he got all the way in and connected, and God got ahold of him.

> But the people blessed by God must persevere no matter what. They must understand that Satan fights the hardest when the greatest spiritual breakthroughs and blessings are just around the corner. Yet, even as the Christ child in Bethlehem was rescued from what seemed to be certain doom, so God will protect and *nurture* his chosen people.[2]
>
> —Jim Cymbala

Did you see yourself in any of these stories? I am more and more convinced that the church is full of people who sincerely love God with all of their heart yet never fully connect and never go through a transformation process whereby Christ can truly begin to form in them and have His way with their lives. Incredible churches with incredible services can produce feel-ings within people that simply do not translate into life change, connection, growth, and the deep roots needed to sustain life, especially a life that must sail through a storm or two from time to time.

In short, there is more—so much more—but connection and relationship are not as optional as we have been led to believe. They are the very stuff of life, life in the Spirit, and the stuff that is absolutely necessary to live life at the next level.

chapter 5

GOD'S BOOT CAMP: WAX ON, WAX OFF

Blessed are those who dwell in your house;
    they are ever praising you.
Blessed are those whose strength is in you,
    who have set their hearts on pilgrimage.
As they pass through the Valley of Baca [weeping],
    they make it a place of springs;
    the autumn rains also cover it with pools.
They go from strength to strength,
    till each appears before God in Zion.
              —Psalm 84:4–7, NIV, emphasis added

I HAVE A GOOD FRIEND NAMED BILL MASON WHO IS ONE OF THE most gifted piano players I have ever been associated with. He can literally play anything, any time; all he has to hear is the first few notes…and he's there. Pastors and worship leaders love him because he can follow them wherever the Spirit leads them, no matter the style, historical time period, or the key. He can even change the key with a motion of the hand and help usher people into the very presence of God.

One day, Bill and I were talking after a rehearsal, and I said to him, "Bill, what an incredible gift you have to be able to play anything you want, whenever you want. What an incredible gift from God to be able to do that." I could tell by the look on his face that I had said the wrong thing, and then he proceeded to enlighten me regarding this precious "gift."

"Gift! Gift?" Bill replied with a smile. "This ain't no gift. You know how I received this gift? When all of the other kids were out playing or going to

31

their sports practices, I was in my room practicing my piano. When all of the teenagers would go out after school, I was in the music room practicing my piano. When the rest of the world went about their lives doing whatever they do, I would be practicing my piano hour upon hour, days upon days, months upon months, and year after year." He explained, "There isn't anything I can do that anybody else could not do if they took the same course of action I did."

Now, Bill was not bragging, and he was not understating the role of God in his talent; in fact, it was his love for God that propelled him on during those early years. He longed to give his gifts back to God to be used. Now when Bill plays, his praise is not a labor. It comes easily. When he worships, it is not difficult. It flows. When he is under the direction of an anointed leader, he is not merely following; he is helping usher that moment into the very presence of God. What an incredible thing to be able to do.

BEING USABLE

So many people, when talking about the mighty things David did, want to point to his achievements and his triumphs as if they happened supernaturally in a vacuum. While the Lord gave him victory, God used his skill and training to prepare him for his moments of triumph. For example, we talk about what an incredible miracle and act of courage it was when David slew Goliath. We talk about his ability to persevere under incredible scrutiny while being chased by Saul. Then we talk about his incredible psalms and his legacy as a good and faithful king, but I want to challenge you to look deeper. He killed Goliath with one stone, but it was one of thousands that he had sent slinging at targets over several years of practice while protecting the sheep. He was an expert slingshot operator before he ever landed that famous throw in that incredibly historic moment. David's ability to persevere under incredible scrutiny was learned over years and years of protecting sheep from predators and bandits in the field. Long before the challenge of adversity came his way, he learned about God's faithfulness and His protection in those long, lonely hours in the pasture with the sheep. As for the psalms, many were written on his heart during those long nights alone as a shepherd boy. He practiced for hours on his harp—the very skill that would bring him into the presence of the king in later years. Lastly, David learned what it meant to be a good king from that same pasture with those same sheep. It turns out that the same skills necessary to be a good shepherd were the ones needed to be a good king. He learned about borders, protection, providing food and water, and caring for the sheep. He led in such a way that would cause others to trust and follow.

Do you see it? This is how God has worked for centuries. We want the mantle right now, the mission right now, the blessing right now, and the ministry right now, but God says in return to learn to play the piano. Learn the importance of waxing on and waxing off. Do you remember the movie from years ago called *The Karate Kid*? It is a great movie with a good theme. One of the messages in the movie is the importance of developing skills that, while appearing to be unrelated to the goal, are essential to preparation for the dream.

Mr. Miyagi was asked to train the boy in karate so that the boy could defend himself from the town bully. So, what is the first thing Mr. Miyagi has the boy to do? He has him paint his wall. Then, when the boy finishes painting and is thoroughly frustrated, he is asked to wax Mr. Miyagi's car. Well, this just throws the boy into a tizzy because he can't see how this has anything to do with his bully or with karate. The moral of the story is that in the development of these basic skills, the boy learns the basics of self-defense—wax on, wax off, block high, block low, block side, and so on.

Pick any number of Bible heroes, and the method is the same. For Moses it was forty years in a desert. For David, as I mentioned before, it was years and years in the pasture with the sheep and then many years on the run testing his character. For the disciples, it was being a fisherman, a tax collector, a doctor. For Jesus, it was carpentry.

Here is what I want you to grasp: Jesus was the Messiah. David was a king. Moses was the leader that led his people out of captivity. Abraham was the father of many nations. The prophets were prophets, and Paul was the revolutionary follower of Christ who would write most of the New Testament. This is who they were. Billy Graham is a world-renowned evangelist. Michael W. Smith is an incredible singer and songwriter. Darlene Zschech is an incredible worship leader. Israel Houghton is a revolutionary Christian songwriter and worship leader. I could go on and on and on, but here is what I want you to grasp: none of these people were ever something else first and then became what they are today or who they became in the Bible. No! They were always who they were going to become all along; they were just in training for that until they became it officially.

You may be mumbling any of the following: Huh? What? Repeat that, please. You lost me. Add your own words to this list. Let me break it down. David was never a shepherd; he was a king in training. Moses was never a shepherd in the desert; he was in training to be the leader of the Hebrew nation. The disciples were never just what their professions were, they were disciples in training. You are not who you think you are. You are the person God created you to be—in training. Problem is, like the karate kid, you need to quit fighting your circumstances and commit to the discipline of wax on, wax off.

The secret to getting all God has for you is not found in a new and better job. It is not in starting some new ministry or some new hobby. The secret is simply this: draw near to God, and do what God has given to you to do right now, right where you are, as if He were watching your every move—because He is.

If you will commit to this, He will absolutely direct your steps and bring the changes into your life in His due time and your due season.

> Trust in the LORD with all your heart,
> And lean not on your own understanding;
> In all your ways acknowledge Him,
> And He shall direct your paths.
>
> —Proverbs 3:5–6

It is impossible to see what He sees for your life looking through human eyes. You must draw near so that over time, as you grow and as Christ is formed in you, you will begin to see what He sees, hear what He hears, and do what He would do. When admonishing and correcting the church in Galatia, Paul stated:

But it is good to be zealous in a good thing always, and not only when
I am present with you. My little children, for whom I labor in birth
again *until Christ is formed in you*.
—Galatians 4:18–19, emphasis added

Paul expressed his frustration to the church he had birthed, because the
people continued to be ruled by their flesh and by their own human logic.
How Paul longed to see Christ formed in them so that who they were would
look a lot more like Christ and what they did would reflect the influence of
Christ more than their flesh.

...that the God of our Lord Jesus Christ, the Father of glory, may give
to you the spirit of wisdom and revelation in the knowledge of Him,
the eyes of your understanding being enlightened; that you may know what is the
hope of His calling, what are the riches of the glory of His inheritance
in the saints, and what is the exceeding greatness of His power toward
us who believe, according to the working of His mighty power.
—Ephesians 1:17–19, emphasis added

True next-level living is commitment to a process, but it is also so much
more. It is trusting God with His plans and His timetable. That's a tough
one for many of us, but we have to grasp the reality that before He can
use us, He has to make us into His image and into the person we will
need to be to make it once we are there. Make sense? Chances are, the
person you are right now is not the person you will need to be to fulfill
your mission any more than a raw recruit is on his first day of boot camp.
A boot-camp recruit is a soldier, yes, because that is who he will become,
but until he becomes it, he is a soldier in training for his sake, for the sake
of those he is called to represent, and for those who must depend upon
him in the field.

He took the disciples with him and had discussions daily in the lecture
hall of Tyrannus. This went on for two years, so that all the Jews and
Greeks who lived in the province of Asia heard the word of the Lord.
—Acts 19:9–10, NIV

Simply put, God is the potter, and we are the clay—you are the clay. God will allow you to jump off the wheel or never even get on it. He will even allow you to fashion yourself into anything you want to be, but what you will become will not bear His mark or look anything like what He has in mind for you. The real problem is that Satan is a potter too, and he has his ideas for what he wants you to look like, and he will do all he can to keep you off God's wheel and on his. The choice is completely yours, and once again you are confronted with a narrow set of options should you choose God's wheel—or anything you want on Satan's. Who will you be fashioned by? Who will shape you? Who will make you into what you will become for the rest of your life?

Let me close this chapter with another story about my friend Don Norris. Don and I have known each other for several years, and I worked with his wife during my years as a school administrator. Don was a crotchety old guy with a loud voice and a "bull-in-a-china-closet" kind of personality, but Don loved the Lord, and through the years he had grown a bit frustrated with God and with others because of his inability to find his place of ministry within the kingdom. Have any of you ever felt like that? Have you ever felt like you were so ready to serve, so willing to do anything and go anywhere, but nobody seemed interested in giving you a chance? Well, that would pretty much describe Don.

I went to lunch with Don one day, and he walked me through the storied history of his life. There had been many ups and downs through the years, but one thing emerged in that conversation that I did not give much thought to that day, but over the next few years it came to hold incredible meaning. Don had worked in factories and industrial complexes most of his adult life at every level you can imagine, and in doing so, he had to learn everything there was to know about constructing and maintaining buildings, factories, and the like. He did it so long that he became involved at the management level, working with city contracts, inspectors, and every facet of building design, maintenance, and remodeling up until the day he retired.

About two years ago, Don had pretty much reached the height of his frustration with the church and Christians in general. He tried everything, but no one seemed to want his help or had any need for the things he was willing to do.

Then, all of a sudden, something very profound happened that would forever alter the course of Don's life. Don, almost on a whim, went on a missions trip to the nation of Peru with a missions organization that was connected to our school. Wouldn't you know that while he was there, they just happened to visit a few sites where construction projects were being planned and some were underway. Don instantly recognized basic problems they were having and noticed they were doing some things in a way that he knew could be done better and cheaper. The missions organization leader instantly saw something that no one had seen before—the perfect need for Don's skill set. Don saw it too, and in a matter of weeks, Don was named the construction manager for this missions organization. Today, he is one the happiest, most fulfilled men you would ever meet. I have even found Don sitting in rooms with his headset on, learning to speak Spanish! All of this at sixty-something years young!

I had a chance to speak with Don some time later, and he told me a few things that I believe are very profound, especially as they relate to the topic I am addressing in this chapter. I remember him telling me with tears in his eyes that when he found his special calling—a mission that required his DNA (just for him)—that all of a sudden, everything he had done that he thought had nothing to do with ministry at all suddenly made sense. He regretted the years he had anguished over not being able to do "ministry," not realizing that God was preparing him for an incredible work.

Now Don builds orphanages, churches, medical clinics, and a whole slew of other things that are bringing about major revolution for Christ in the country of Peru! Don is a missionary! But what I want you to learn is that Don has always been a missionary—in training—and not a construction manager at city buildings and plants. God sees the whole picture, beginning to end. While we cannot see the end, we know the One who holds our days in the palm of His hand. Can you trust Him with the end? Can you trust Him with where you are right now and everything in between? If the answer is yes, then get on the wheel, stay on the wheel, and let the Master Potter make you into something incredibly useful in the kingdom. Do what you can in the natural, and then wait on God to do the supernatural. He will, if you will let Him. Will you let Him?

Spend a moment right now and walk through your prayer cycle—ACTS. Talk to Him about what you have learned today. Journal what He says back to you, and commit to a very simple thing—wax on, wax off.

> Many a man claims to have unfailing love, but a faithful man who can find?
>
> —Proverbs 20:6, NIV

SECTION 2

PURIFICATION—PLACED SQUARELY IN THE HANDS OF THE MASTER POTTER

Seek the LORD while he may be found;
  call on him while he is near.
Let the wicked forsake his way
  and the evil man his thoughts. . . .
so it is my word that goes out from my mouth:
  It will not return to me empty,
but will accomplish what I desire
  and achieve the purpose for which I sent it.
                              —Isaiah 55:6–7, 11, NIV

chapter 6

ILLUMINATION

This is the message we have heard from him and declare to you:
God is light; in him there is no darkness at all. If we claim to
have fellowship with him yet walk in the darkness, we lie and
do not live by the truth. But if we walk in the light, as he is in
the light, we have fellowship with one another, and the blood of
Jesus his Son, purifies us from all sin.

—1 John 1:5–7, NIV

He will bring to light what is hidden in darkness and will
expose the motives of men's hearts.

—1 Corinthians 4:5, NIV

AFTER YOU UNDERSTAND AND SENSE THE URGENCY TO WAKE UP
and begin to do the work of relationship, you will no doubt begin
to experience God's presence and begin to hear His voice. This is
not just theory, but it is a promise from Scripture. The Book of Jeremiah
makes it very clear that as you draw near to Him, He will in turn draw near
to you, even confide in you according to Psalm 25. We have gone over all of
that in the past chapters. If you are faithful daily, you will begin to experience God more and more each day.

As you draw near, something amazing will begin to happen. As you place
your focus squarely on Him, you will begin to experience "illumination," which
basically means "light." Scripture refers again and again to the concept of light
and darkness and always in reference to spiritual awareness and being able to
see things clearly that before you were unable to see. This is a natural outcome
of spiritual growth and maturity. Ephesians says it like this:

> For you were once darkness, but now you are light in the Lord. Live as children of light…and find out what pleases the Lord. Have nothing to do with the fruitless deeds of darkness, but rather expose them. For it is shameful even to mention what the disobedient do in secret. But everything exposed by the light becomes visible.… This is why it is said: "*Wake up, O sleeper*, rise from the dead, and Christ will shine on you."
>
> —Ephesians 5:8, 10–14, NIV, emphasis added

Notice the urgency of the hour and the reference to waking up—the same message as the first section of this book.

Jesus, when speaking from heaven to Saul (who would later become Paul) on the road to Damascus, said this:

> I am sending you to them to open their eyes and turn them from darkness to light, and from the power of Satan to God, so that they may receive forgiveness of sins and a place among those who are sanctified by faith in me.
>
> —Acts 26:17–18, NIV

This is a passage where Paul is speaking to the believers in Rome:

> And do this, knowing the time, that now it is high time to *awake out of sleep*; for now our salvation is nearer than when we first believed. The night is far spent, the day is at hand. Therefore let us cast off the works of darkness, and let us put on the armor of light. Let us walk properly, as in the day, not in revelry and drunkenness, not in lewdness and lust, not in strife and envy. But put on the Lord Jesus Christ, and make no provision for the flesh, to fulfill its lusts.
>
> —Romans 13:11–14, emphasis added

Do you see the pattern in Scripture? There is this call to shift your focus off of the stuff you are doing—good or bad—and to turn your focus onto Him, or to "put on the Lord Jesus Christ" as Paul says. Then, a natural outcome of that "waking up" and shifting of focus (drawing near) is that you begin to walk in the light as He is in the light. Simply put, you turn on the light. Now, hang in there with me because we are going somewhere with this in a minute.

THE LIGHT THAT HEALS

Billy Graham was once approached by several very prominent evangelical Christian leaders and was challenged about his stance on many controversial social issues, such as abortion, homosexuality, and others. These well-meaning leaders asked why Billy would not do more and speak out more and be a part of the battle to preserve our Christian values here in America.

The story goes on to say that Billy thought for a second and then turned and answered his critics and colleagues in his usual humble yet profound way. He said this: "Some people are called to fight the darkness. But my calling is different...while some are no doubt called to fight the darkness, I have been called to turn on the light."

What an incredibly profound and timely thought. God is calling all of us to turn on the light for others and in our own daily walk with Christ. We must get all the way in and allow the Lord to light our path so that we might be able to see where we are going clearly, not with human eyes and human understanding but with our spiritual eyes and senses.

Imagine for a moment having to walk across a very crowded and cluttered warehouse that has sharp objects, things to trip over, and no long aisles or paths. Now, imagine walking across that room from one end to the other with the lights completely off—total darkness. Imagine the stumbling, the frustration, the disappointment, and the sense of futility. Well, that sounds like many Christians I encounter both as a pastor and just in the daily comings and goings in the kingdom. Why is that? Why would God's people experience such things when we have so much light within our reach? The answer is that there are far too many of us who love Jesus but choose to live in the dark about who He is, His ways, and His will for our lives. It is also because so many have chosen to stay at the play, to slumber, and to do everything but relationship.

43

I have attached a diagram that I think illustrates the concept of darkness and light. Take a look at it for a moment, and then we will look at its implications for your life.

Darkness and Light Illustrated

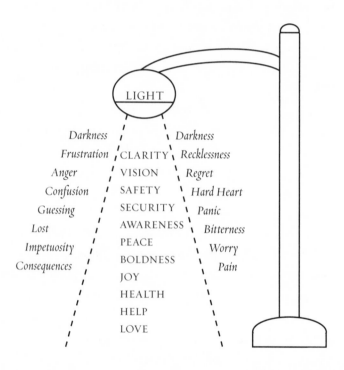

Now, let's talk about some of the implications of this light. What you see above is meant to represent a simple streetlight. I can remember playing hide-and-seek for hours in front of our house when I was young, and I can still see very clearly in my mind that light post that was "base." This was the post where the person who was "it" would count to two hundred by fives and then come looking for us. I loved that game.

Well, the diagram above is meant to represent being in or out of God's will. The more you are in the center of God's will for your life, the more in the center of the light you are. Conversely, the more outside of God's will you are, the more outside the light you are. So the light represents life in God's will, being under His protection, having the ability to see clearly, and experiencing an illuminated life. The darkness represents a life lived outside the will of God—Christian or non-Christian.

That's right, I said Christian or non-Christian. The fact is, God will let you walk outside that light, just as He has many a great Christian in the past. On that list of those He has let walk outside the light are:

- Adam and Eve: God allowed them to eat of the tree even though He had clearly said not to.

- Abraham: He had sex with his wife's handmaiden and later took a detour to Egypt.

- Moses: He murdered a man in a fight and then fled the scene.

- The entire nation of Israel: The Israelites would not cross over and possess the land, resulting in forty years in the wilderness.

- David: He committed adultery, murder, and more.

- Solomon: *Wow!* Is there anything he didn't do?

- The people of God throughout biblical history: Again and again they have followed after false gods.

- The church at Corinth: Man, they were even having religious, ceremonial sex with prostitutes.

- Peter: He denied Christ three times.

- Paul: While we do not know exactly what he did, we do know he said the following:

I do not understand what I do. For what I want to do I do not do, but what I hate I do. And if I do what I do not want to do, I agree that the law is good. As it is, it is no longer I myself who do it, but it is sin living in me. I know that nothing good lives in me, that is, in my sinful nature. For I have the desire to do what is good, but I cannot carry it out.

—Romans 7:15–18, NIV

God will absolutely let you walk outside the light. He will even let you live there for a season, but not without a cost to you or to someone you love, and never without the conviction of the Holy Spirit nipping at your heels and messing with your sleep.

I often get asked to lead sessions that last several weeks on issues that parents face while raising their children. Usually for week three's session, I use a woman to assist me in speaking about issues related to female medical and physiological issues. Several years ago, I was scheduled to speak to a group of parents, but for this particular week, I was unable to secure the person I would normally take with me. Instead, I asked the school nurse, who was a very good friend, to accompany me for this session.

As we traveled to the meeting, small talk turned to talk about some very personal issues in her life and about her marriage. The drive to the event took about an hour, but about forty-five minutes into the drive, she told me that she was leaving her husband, had been flirting with thoughts of a relationship with other men, and fully believed it was all God's will. She spoke of how happy her children (elementary to college age) were that she and her husband were finally divorcing and how she simply believed that it was her turn to be happy. She talked about how disappointed she was that her husband was not a spiritual man or leader in their home, and she spoke of how unhappy she had become in her marriage and of all the things her husband simply had stopped doing for several years. More than anything else, she made it abundantly clear that she was done. It was over, and nothing in heaven or earth could change that. The papers were drawn up; everything was planned legally and logistically. They were already living in different rooms, so all that was left was for him to move out later that week.

Man, I was looking for the nearest exit. I wanted to turn the car around and go back home. I didn't know what to do. Now, I know that many of you are thinking that I never should have started down the road in a car with her by myself, and I would never do that today, but at that time in my life and in this situation, it just did not seem like any big deal. Lesson learned.

Anyway, since we were almost at the venue, and since I knew there was already gathered a room full of excited and eager parents, I decided to proceed, but for the last ten minutes of that ride, I was sick. I was sick not only at what I had heard but also in knowing that in about half an hour she was going to be speaking to this room full of parents. I knew that before God, she was undone and living clearly outside that light. Worse yet, as we rode and I listened, I said nothing—no rebuke, no questioning. I was just in shock and was just sick in my spirit.

Again, I know now that I should have been stronger and just told her that I was not going to allow her to speak that night because of the state of her life and the testimony of her confession, but somehow I rationalized and reasoned my way into allowing her to proceed. I told myself that she was not going to be speaking about spiritual matters but rather medical and physiological matters only, so I relented and allowed her to speak, and she was great. She did a fantastic job and was very much appreciated by all those parents of daughters, but I writhed in anguish with each passing moment, feeling that I was somehow betraying the God of the universe for allowing her any voice at all with these Christian parents.

Well, somehow we got through that hour and a half, but by then, all I could think was that I have about an hour ride home to muster the courage to speak up. She was several years older than I was, and at that time, this helped build the intimidation I was feeling, but as we rode back, she started in again, talking about the same thing. For the first ten minutes, I sat silent, again searching for the right words and waiting for the right opportunity.

I had just about resolved myself to just getting her back to her car and getting out of there when she said those magic words. "I am so thankful God is orchestrating this and that He is going to walk with me through this to better things." That was it. The spirit man in me had heard all he could hear, and right then and there, I stopped my friend dead in her tracks and said, "You are wrong." This caught her off guard and she replied, "Excuse me?" Then the Holy Spirit just took over.

Over the next forty minutes I dismantled her entire divorce theology, and I had a response for every grenade she was able to lob my way. The biggest thing I had going for me was that she really believed herself to be a Christian, which I believe she was. This would turn out to be the greatest asset

I had as I learned that she absolutely cared about what the Lord thought about her and what His response would be.

After the next forty minutes, we found ourselves parked next to her car, and she was pretty frustrated with me. In those next few moments, God moved heaven and earth for that woman and for that precious family. He gave me the words to say to her. They may not have been 100 percent herme-neutically, theologically textbook correct, but they were the words God gave me in the moment I needed them most.

I said to my friend, "Mary, God will absolutely allow you to go where you want to go, but you need to understand that He will not go there with you. You want to leave your husband, pursue relationships with other men, and have Him bless you to boot? You don't see how deceived you are right now, but believe me when I tell you that you have been deceived." (Now she was really mad!) I continued, "You can go there [outside the light], but He will not go there with you. You go alone, and you drag each of your children right out there with you to face all of the stuff children and adult children of divorce face, and they will hurt and suffer for your disobedience."

Wow, was it quiet, and wow, was she mad—visibly mad but not defiant. That was what was most amazing and what told me there was an ounce of hope. Then she turned to me and said through gritted teeth, "So what am I supposed to do?" I could see years of disappointment, discouragement, and longing in her eyes that only years of neglect, unappreciation, and a loveless marriage can cause.

Nevertheless, I looked at her and replied, "Mary, here is all that I am saying. Do you love the Lord and want to be in His will?" She said, "Yes." Then I said, "Then I am just going to ask you to do one thing. Please, just this one thing."

She looked at me, part glaring and part hurting. "What?" she mustered with just a shred of possibility in her voice. I replied, "When you get home tonight, when you pull the car in the driveway, I simply ask that you turn the car off, sit quietly for a moment, look God in the eye, and in the stillness of that moment, ask Him what He wants you to do." Then I said, "I believe with all my heart, that if you ask Him *tonight*, He will tell you, but then it will be up to you to decide what to do with what He tells you."

I will never forget the look on her face when she said, "OK." It was as if she knew she was miles outside the light and her last chance at a rescue rope had just been thrown in her direction. I believe that in her heart of hearts, as much as she wanted change, as much as she wanted to be loved, and as much as she wanted for this chapter in her life to be over, she also knew down deep that this could mean her relationship with Christ would be severed, possibly irreparably. She had reached such a point of desperation that it was a risk she was willing to take with the one and only life she had to live—a life cancer had almost taken from her years before.

Well, she left and went her way that night, and I know that you all can rebuke me and criticize me for ever taking that ride in the first place. I could tell you it was a different time and a different era and a perfectly innocent situation, but the fact is that my time with Mary that night was absolutely God ordained, and the miracle He wrought over the next weeks and months is nothing short of a Holy Ghost intervention.

She did go home that night, and in her driveway she said the words she promised she would say. According to Mary, she felt conviction, but only a little (which was a significant improvement), and then even went so far as to challenge God by laying a fleece out for Him. She and her husband were still living in the same house but in separate rooms. She knew that her husband, without fail, would always be asleep with the door closed by 9:00 sharp every night! She told God, "All right, God, if he is up and looks like he has been waiting for me to come home, I will at least speak to him, but that's it!" Then she got out of her car and walked in the house, sure the lights would be out and his door closed so she could at last feel like she had done all I asked and could move on, but God had other plans.

As she went up the stairs, there he was, sitting on the edge of his bed, waiting for her to come home. Right then (and this, I believe, really speaks to her spiritual condition, even in the midst of her sin), she said that her heart melted a little, and she walked in and said to him, "Joe, I don't even know why, but if you will go to a counselor with me, I will at least not leave yet." He broke down. He had been trying to reconcile for weeks but to no avail.

Here is the real kicker. One of her biggest issues with Joe was that he would not go to church with her or have anything to do with spiritual matters, even as they related to the kids. This was one of the main reasons Mary wanted to leave Joe. As crazy as that sounds, there are hundreds of women who want desperately to be married to a man who is as in love with Jesus and as committed a Christian as they are. Well, it just so happened that while God brought Mary to me for this supernatural moment in time, the weekend before, Joe had attended a Promise Keepers event in Southern California and had given his life to Christ and wanted so much to tell Mary about what the Lord was doing in his life.

That night, Joe and Mary sat up and talked for a long time. While they were not reconciled overnight, they felt strong enough to get their children out of bed at about 2:00 in the morning to tell them that they were not splitting up and that they were committing to piece their marriage back together. To Mary's amazement, her children broke down and wept with joy; even her son who was a senior in high school wept openly, overcome with joy and relief.

Last summer, Mary and Joe celebrated their thirty-fifth wedding anniversary. They are more in love today than ever, are following the Lord, and are grateful for one night outside the light, when they chose to walk back into the light and be forever changed as a result.

God has so much for you in that light. Satan will do all he can to entice you, deceive you, and lure you out of the light and into the darkness. Don't be fooled. Don't be deceived. Move to the center, and then watch to see what God does with your faithfulness. Experience His provision, His protection, and His direction. The choice is yours—right and wrong. You decide.

> Hear, O LORD, my righteous plea;
> listen to my cry.
> Give ear to my prayer—

it does not rise from deceitful lips.
May my vindication come from you;
    may your eyes see what is right.
Though you probe my heart and examine me at night,
    though you test me, you will find nothing;
    I have resolved that my mouth will not sin.
                    —Psalm 17:1–3, NIV

Allow Him to shine His light anywhere He chooses, and then allow Him to do an incredible work with whatever that light may find. Light reveals anything and everything the Lord wants you to see. Surrender everything to it, and allow Him to purify the secret places. Don't be like the rich young ruler. Give Him anything, anytime, any root He chooses—let Him have it, and let Him make something beautiful out of the very thing Satan meant for evil.

chapter 7

PURIFICATION 1:
THE LIGHT OF SELF-REVELATION

God has given us his Spirit. That's why we don't think the same way
that the people of this world think.

— 1 Corinthians 2:12, CEV

I N SCRIPTURE, ONE OF THE MOST PROFOUND STORIES IS THE STORY
of the rich young ruler. Many people read right over this story, thinking
it is an admonishment only for the very wealthy, but the underlying
theme of this timeless story is one that applies to all of us who dare go
deeper with the Lord. When the rich young ruler came to Jesus, he was
not only desiring to know Him as Savior, but he also wanted very much to
be a follower of Christ. In his earnest questioning for what he had to do
(works) to be a perfect Christian, he was met with an answer that created
what Henry Blackaby in *Experiencing God* calls a "crisis of belief."[1]

> The young man said to Him [referring to the list of commandments Jesus
> said he needed to keep], "All these things I have kept from my youth.
> What do I still lack?" Jesus said to him, "If you want to be perfect, go, sell
> what you have and give to the poor, and you will have treasure in heaven;
> and come, follow Me." But when the young man heard that saying, he
> went away sorrowful, for he had great possessions.
>
> — Matthew 19:20–22

One of the most critical parts of your journey to the next level is about to
occur. It is a place in the journey where many a strong man or woman has
stopped, choosing not to go on to the deeper things of God, much like that
wealthy young man. For every person who has decided to follow Jesus into

the deeper things, there comes a place where he or she will begin to experience the kind of illumination I spoke of in the last chapter. As the light begins to come on, it is very exciting. Even your Bible reading feels different. As you read Scripture, it begins to read and examine you. Your prayer life becomes richer, and worship and church become more meaningful. You begin to see the Lord working in you, through you, and all around you.

Then, all of a sudden, God begins to direct that light to the specific things He wants you to see about yourself. Now, this isn't exactly what you thought you signed up for back at ground zero when you began this journey, but nevertheless, here you are, confronted with your own rich-young-ruler experience. Although your issue may not necessarily be money, it will be something you value or are holding on to tightly. Here is what will occur first. God is going to take that light and shine it on places in your past that you have not fully dealt with—places that still hold you captive and things that you are carrying that you must let go of before you can go on with God.

There is a saying that is very popular but also very deceptive. It says, "Time heals all wounds." Well, time does not heal all wounds—never has and never will. Time provides distance from the event or the relationship. With time comes forgetting, with forgetting comes a new focus, and with a new focus comes layer upon layer of dirt over a wound that lies open beneath the surface. For some wounds, a root begins to develop that is invisible to the naked eye but grows stronger every day.

Here are a few examples of the power of a buried root. Did you know that one of the most important relationships on this earth for good or bad is the relationship between a father and his daughter? Did you know that a girl's sense of security and self-worth comes directly from the father? And here is the kicker: did you know that a girl's view of her father, if left buried beneath the surface, will determine her view of men in general for her entire adult life?

Did you know that a boy's concept of his father will be his view and his concept of God and authority? Moms, did you know the way you train or allow (there's a difference) your son to treat you and interact with you over the years will be the way he treats and interacts with his wife?

Roots grow deep—far deeper than we think. We can allow the things of the past to influence everything we do in the future if all we do is bury them. That is absolutely contrary to God's plan for your life. You see, God wants to be the One who influences every decision, every interaction, and every relationship you ever have from here on, but He can't lift you to that height if you insist upon staying tethered to your roots.

When I get to this part of the seminar or class, I always like to challenge my classes with this simple question: "What's your but...?" Or, in other words, when you talk to God, what is your, "Lord, I will do anything but _____." Or, "Lord, I will deal with anyone but _____." Or, "Lord, I can forgive everything but _____." Or, "Lord, I simply do not want to talk about _____." Whatever thing you are holding on to, whatever thing keeps you from completely giving God everything, doing anything for Him, ministering to whomever He assigns you, or dealing with whatever secret thing, you can rest assured that is the very thing He will say must be dealt with—first, before you can go one step further.

You have come too far to turn back now. Allow me, over the next few pages, to walk you through the process that will start you down the path to the past just for a brief season so that you can bring healing where there are open wounds and mend bridges where there is only destruction and aftermath.

> Who can understand his errors?
> Cleanse me from secret faults.
> Keep back Your servant also from presumptuous sins;
> Let them not have dominion over me.
> Then I shall be blameless,
> And I shall be innocent of great transgression.
> —Psalm 19:12–13

WHAT'S YOUR *BUT*?

Now, I will tell you this: for most people—not all, but most—when they are confronted with this whole concept or they read the questions with the blanks, a name, a situation, or a place comes to mind immediately. Others will need to spend some time in prayer, asking God to shine the light and reveal whether or not they are clear and free of anything that would hinder them in their walk with God. With that said, here is a sample list of the kinds of things that tend to weigh people down or keep us in the grip of fear, condemnation, guilt, anger, or depression:

- Broken relationship with a close friend
- Abuse suffered at the hands of another
- Abuse against another
- Deep hurt by a mother or father
- A broken relationship with a sibling
- A broken romantic relationship
- Infidelity
- Betrayal
- An abortion
- Debt owed to someone
- Awaiting repayment of a debt
- Unfaithfulness to spouse
- Unconfessed sin in the past

LOOKING BACK TO MOVE FORWARD

These are just a sampling, but hopefully there are enough memory joggers above to spark a memory where one is needed. Now, here is the crux of the point: this is not to simply drudge up the past, but it is absolutely to say that you cannot hold unforgiveness, bitterness, or a callous heart and think that you can still become tender with God in all other areas of your life. Until it is dealt with, it will forever have its grip on you and will affect decisions you make, relationships you form, and the amount of love you are willing to give.

> If we say that we have no sin, we deceive ourselves, and the truth is not in us. If we confess our sins, He is faithful and just to forgive us our sins and to cleanse us from all unrighteousness. If we say that we have not sinned, we make Him a liar, and His word is not in us.
>
> —1 John 1:8–10

The goal here is simply this: By allowing God to help you *re*member, you can go back and *dis*member or take that situation or relationship apart piece by piece in order to examine it thoroughly. You can then see all its parts, fix what is broken, and offer it up to God as something that no longer has power over you. Praise God!

When you do this, and I mean really do this, something amazing will happen. I guarantee it. An incredibly profound event will take place in the depths of your understanding about who you are, and you will begin to discover that these things in your past, after submitting them to the Lord, will literally go from being the things that once weighed you down to the very things that will bring you strength, victory, and (here's the best one) make you completely usable by God. God will take what Satan meant for evil and use it for good! Praise God!

> And a voice spoke to him [Peter] again the second time, "What God has cleansed you must not call common."
>
> —Acts 10:15

I know this has been a lot to swallow all at once, and there is no telling what kinds of things are swirling around in your head right now. Maybe I have opened up an old wound or two, but believe me when I tell you that if it hurts, it is not an old wound. It is an open, unhealed sore—an open wound buried beneath inches of dirt.

In the next chapter, we will go deeper and really begin to do the work of repair and restoration, but for now, just find a way to be still before God and allow Him to reveal to you anything and everything that is left undone, anything lying behind that is entangling you. Allow Him to shine that light anywhere and everywhere. Just be honest with Him. Then, like my friend in the car that night, tell Him you will do what He wants you to do. Then watch for your deliverance.

Deliverance is yours, and it is coming, because the end result is simple. The goal is not to live here in this place of remembering but rather to cut that net that entangles you once and for all, so you can do as Paul commands in Philippians:

> Brethren, I do not count myself to have apprehended; but one thing I do, forgetting those things which are behind and reaching forward to those things which are ahead, I press toward the goal for the prize of the upward call of God in Christ Jesus.
>
> —Philippians 3:13–14

chapter 8

PURIFICATION 2: WHAT'S HOLDING YOU DOWN

I am the true vine, and My Father is the vinedresser. Every branch in Me that does not bear fruit He takes away; and every branch that bears fruit He prunes, that it may bear more fruit.

—John 15:1–2

O UR HOME CHURCH ALL THROUGH THE 1990S WAS A WONDERFUL church in Orange County, California, called Mariners Church. It was a large, nondenominational church in the coastal Newport Beach area. Some of the most significant discoveries and moves of God in my life occurred during those years at Mariners. By far, my favorite event each year was the annual men's retreat held at the world famous Forest Home campgrounds. This, I believe, is one of the most spiritual places on earth. Every March, for about eight years, it was the place where God met me face-to-face and spoke to me. Every year, we would have powerful praise and worship, incredible Spirit-led preaching and teaching, and moments alone with the Lord in the beautiful San Bernardino Mountains.

Of all the years that I attended, one year stands out among the others as the most memorable, but it didn't start out that way. First, there was no guest speaker. Our pastor, Kenton Beshore, was slated to be the facilitator, which was great, but I did look forward to hearing a different voice for those few days each year. While I knew Kenton would have a strong word, on the first night Kenton announced that he really wouldn't be doing much speaking and that we were going to do more quiet time, journaling, and getting out in nature. The letdown I felt was enormous. I didn't just look forward to this weekend every year, I came limping in, needing a refilling, a cleansing, and a whole spiritual makeover. So when he said we were going to do it differently that year, I was not too excited, and I wasn't alone in that feeling.

But, like everyone else, we knew this was our pastor, and if this was the course he would have us go that weekend, we believed it came from the Lord. Rather than fight it or be discouraged, we decided to do exactly as directed, hoping for the best.

Oh, my Lord! Over the next few days, in my quiet times and in my times out on the trail or sitting by the creek, the Lord moved over me as never before. In fact, it was there that I charted the outline for a new seminar I would be teaching at church called "Next Level Parenting." This would later become the basis and outline for my second book, *Next Level Parenting*, due out in the next few years. Suffice it to say, while there was no flesh-and-blood speaker that weekend, God still spoke to our hearts in ways I had not experienced in all my years there.

The most amazing part of the entire retreat happened on the final morning, Sunday morning. This was always testimony morning, and it was one of the few things that stayed on the schedule. There were several powerful testimonies, followed by manly applause and cheers, kind of like a football game or something. Then something extraordinary happened. God came down and took over that room in an incredible and miraculous way. How'd He do it? He did it through one humble, broken man, who, after looking his God in the face, had decided he could no longer look his brothers in the eye until he came clean.

I will never forget when this man stood up, walked to the microphone, stood silently for a moment, and then tearfully said, "Hi. The Lord told me that I needed to confess something this morning, and so I am going to do that right now." The tears began to really flow, and you could hear a pin drop in that room of over five hundred men. He continued, "I am addicted to pornography, and I have not been able to stop for two years now." We all began to break, and before long, there was not a dry eye in the building.

"I am scared to death right now, not because of anything I have done. God will forgive me for that; in fact, He already has. That is what this weekend has done for me, but what I am scared of the most is what you all will think of me now that you know the real me." Now, even our pastor, Kenton, was tearing up as we all somehow sensed the magnitude of that moment. How many men was he speaking for that morning? How many were secretly thinking, "Me too"? How many wish they had the courage this young man had?

The man concluded, "I don't know what you all will think of me now. I only know that I can't make it and stay true to my new commitment without your help." Then there was a long pause. The only sound was that of the sniffles and sobs heard around the room. "So I am asking for your forgiveness, your friendship, and your help. Thank you."

In an instant, as if we had rehearsed it for weeks, we were all on our feet, wildly applauding and yelling as if rallying a battle cry on a foreign battlefield. Many of the men near him and those who came with him that weekend engulfed him in their arms—arms full of mercy, grace, and love. In an instant, guilt was defeated, condemnation was sent screaming out of the room, and fear no longer held him fast. For the first time, perhaps in years, this precious child of God knew what it meant to be free. The truth had truly set him free.

THE RACE TO THE FINISH LINE

The topic for these two chapters is purification. Each seminar or class that I teach on the topic of purification always involves two visual and experiential components that are both very powerful. First, I use a volunteer from the audience to come and stand on the platform or at the front of the room. Then, I have one strong man come and grab the left leg and hold it down. This man represents guilt. Then I have a second strong man come and hold the other leg down, representing fear. Lastly, I have a third strong person come up and hold the person from behind by the waist, representing condemnation.

Once all of the characters are in place, we read the famous passage from Philippians that we ended the last chapter with:

Brethren, I do not count myself to have apprehended; but one thing I do, forgetting those things which are behind and reaching forward to those things which are ahead, I press toward the goal for the prize of the upward call of God in Christ Jesus.

—Philippians 3:13–14

Then I tell the man who is being held down, "Start running!" Now, of course, the person is completely unable to move an inch. No matter how hard he tries, he cannot move—not as long as guilt, fear, and condemnation have a hold on him. He is unable to move forward. Here is another thing that is interesting: he can still worship with his arms in the air, and he can still stand and enjoy a service. He can eat, drink, and appear normal, even pleasant, from the waist up, as if nothing was wrong, but ask him to move on something. No way. Ask him to try and be a part of an event or something that requires commitment. No can do. When God calls him up higher or to walk down a path with Him, it ain't happening. Can't help it. Guilt, condemnation, and fear are just too strong. Moving forward is simply not an option.

This is even better. He can name it, claim it, rebuke it, speak to it, ignore it, rise above it—you name your best religious phrase—and nothing. All three still have what appears to be a death grip. Why? Because guilt, condemnation, and fear all have roots. They all have an origin that simply will *not* be overlooked or left for dead without a fight, but praise God, the only fighting we have to do is look each of those situations in the eye, have a conversation with the Lord about those things that so easily ensnare us, and then release them to God's trust to do anything He wants to do with them. Sometimes, we find that the very thing we have been trying so hard to forget is the very thing He wants to use to help others.

It turns out that for each of the things that hold us down, there is a promise in the form of a scripture.

Guilt

...and since we have a great priest over the house of God, let us draw near to God with a sincere heart in full assurance of faith, having our hearts sprinkled to cleanse us from a guilty conscience and having our bodies washed with pure water. Let us hold unswervingly to the hope we profess, for he who promised is faithful. And let us consider how we may spur one another on toward love and good deeds.

—Hebrews 10:21–24, NIV

Condemnation

Therefore, there is now no condemnation for those who are in Christ Jesus, because through Christ Jesus the law of the Spirit of life set me free from the law of sin and death. For what the law was powerless to do in that it was weakened by the sinful nature, God did by sending his own Son in the likeness of sinful man to be a sin offering.

—Romans 8:1–3, NIV

Fear

And so we know and rely on the love God has for us. God is love. Whoever lives in love lives in God, and God in him. In this way, love is made complete among us so that we will have confidence on the day of judgment, because in this world we are like him. *There is no fear in love. But perfect love drives out fear,* because fear has to do with punishment. The one who fears is not made perfect in love. We love because he first loved us.

—1 John 4:16–19, NIV, emphasis added

RECKONING, RELINQUISHING, AND RESTORATION

For every undone thing in our past that has a hold on us, there must come a reckoning, a relinquishing, and a restoration. In reckoning, you are open and honest with God about whatever it is that holds you captive. In releasing, there is an action being taken whereby you surrender that thing to the Lord, never to hold it again, never to let it have power or sway over you again. In restoration, you allow the Lord to mend the broken places, broken relationships, or broken self-images. Then you place it in the hands of the Lord, knowing that what Satan meant for evil, God intends to use for good!

MONKEY BARS

The second incredibly symbolic activity that I teach in classes is use an old-fashioned monkey trap. It is crude, barbaric, and primitive but nevertheless incredibly effective and still used in parts of the world. The monkey trap is a type of cage made with bars all around. Each bar is just far enough from the next bar to allow an open hand through. Then, on the inside of this cagelike structure lies the bait—a banana or something else that is attractive to monkeys. Well, it is not long until an unsuspecting monkey comes along who does not know that he is only moments away from sure death—and, oddly enough, it will be a death he chooses based on his actions.

The monkey sticks his innocent little hand through the bars, picks up the bait, and then tries to get his hand out only to discover that the hand will not come out while it keeps its grip on the bait. The problem is that the monkey won't let go of the bait. Even while the captors begin to beat the poor thing, it will not let go of the bait.

Wow! That is so like us. We hold on to things in the past that we need to release, forgive, and leave in God's hands—many times holding on while we get beat up, defeated, and profoundly shaken for years and years to come. All of this, when all we have to do to be free is let go of the bait.

When I close this particular class or service, I always like to ask this simple question, "What has you today?" By that I mean, what is it that you just can't shake? What memory? What person? What circumstance? What has you? Because whatever *has* you literally holds you captive. What holds you captive today?

At the end of the class, I challenge each person to write down anything that might be in their past that has yet to be dealt with, forgiven, or laid at the Master's feet. Then, one by one, each person files by and puts their hand with the paper through the bars, holds the paper in their fist, says a prayer of release or forgiveness of whatever their particular memory is, and then releases it to God, pulling their hand to safety and symbolically declaring that this thing no longer has power over them.

What a powerful visual image. Each person, painstakingly and most of the time with tears running down their cheeks, lets go of years' worth of baggage, hurt, anger, frustration, guilt, condemnation, and fear in exchange for one thing—freedom.

Jeremiah has an incredible promise for whatever has you today:

> Then you will call upon Me and go and pray to Me, and I will listen to you. And you will seek Me and find Me, when you search for Me with all your heart. I will be found by you, says the LORD, *and I will bring you back from your captivity.*
> —Jeremiah 29:12–14, emphasis added

What an incredible promise! He knows! And He has a plan. Draw near. Seek Him with your whole heart. Find Him, and He will bring you back from your captivity! You were made to run, to move, and to finish the race.

> Keep your heart with all diligence,
> For out of it spring the issues of life.
> Put away from you a deceitful mouth,
> And put perverse lips far from you.
> Let your eyes look straight ahead,
> And your eyelids look right before you.
> Ponder the path of your feet,
> And let all your ways be established.
> *Do not turn to the right or the left;*
> *Remove your foot from evil.*
> —Proverbs 4:23–27, emphasis added

Run, man of God, *run*! Run, woman of God, *run*! You were born for this cause, and all of heaven looks on in great anticipation at the great things God will do through you!

LETTING GO—IT'S YOUR TURN

Today, as you enter your prayer time, I want to challenge you to take out a piece of paper and spend a moment reflecting on anything lying behind that you know you need to be freed from or to let go of. Think about this, and allow it to flow through the end of your pen. God knows, and I believe you do as well. Now, what will you do with what you know? Write it down.

Next, take a moment to place that paper in your hand, hold it in your fist, and simply ask the Lord, "What would You have me to do with these?" For some, you will know right away. It is a phone call you must make, a debt you must pay, an apology you need to make, or a person you need to forgive and release. Simply offer it up to Jesus, telling Him one simple thing: "I will do whatever You tell me to do with this." Then drop it. Release it. Let Christ take it from you, never to hold power over you again. Then listen over the next few days and watch to see what God might want you to do.

> Therefore submit to God. Resist the devil and he will flee from you. *Draw near to God and He will draw near to you.* Cleanse your hands, you sinners; and purify your hearts, you double-minded. Lament and mourn and weep! Let your laughter be turned to mourning and your joy to gloom. *Humble yourselves in the sight of the Lord, and He will lift you up.*
> —James 4:7–10, emphasis added

chapter 9

A LIFE LIVED ABOVE AND BELOW GROUND

Who can understand his errors?
Cleanse me from secret faults.
Keep back Your servant also from presumptuous sins;
Let them not have dominion over me.
Then I shall be blameless,
And I shall be innocent of great transgression.
Let the words of my mouth and the meditation of my heart
Be acceptable in Your sight,
O LORD, my strength and my Redeemer.
—Psalm 19:12–14

LET'S GO DEEPER. ONE OF THE MOST COMMON OCCURRENCES I experience when counseling and speaking with people, especially people walking through this purification process, is when folks cannot put a finger on anything specific that has them entangled. They just know they are entangled. What do I mean? Take another look at the lamp illustration. Pay particular attention to the descriptors that lie outside the light; then we will come back and deal with the hidden things—the secret things, the things that are not visible to the naked eye.

Darkness and Light Illustrated

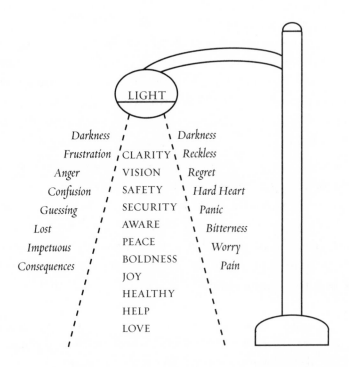

The questions and comments I receive from some folks go something like this: "I cannot tell you exactly what it is in my past, or even my present. All I know is that I experience many of the things that are outside that light." In other words, they don't know what the root is. They have no clue, but fear, anxiety, discouragement, or frustration have them all of the time. One emotion that many deal with is anger. They can be going along just fine, and then something will happen, and they go from zero to rage with the flip of a switch—and they hate that about themselves, but they are powerless to stop it. Proverbs says this:

> The path of the righteous is like the first gleam of dawn,
> shining ever brighter till the full light of day.

> But the way of the wicked is like deep darkness;
>> they do not know what makes them stumble.
>>> —Proverbs 4:18–19, NIV

Now, these folks that I am speaking of are not necessarily wicked; most are incredibly well-meaning followers of Christ, trying desperately to live life at the next level, but what holds them down, what beats them up and defeats them on a daily basis absolutely is wicked, a tool of Satan. Of course, they think they are powerless to stop it. They don't know the root, which begs the question, "What now?"

Remember, this is a spiritual principle that says when you can't make sense of something in the physical realm (by touch, sight, reason, or logic), then something is going on in the spiritual realm. The next principle follows suit and says that you can never combat a spiritual problem with a physical approach. You will never get there. Some of you will never understand the depth of your issue in the natural because it must be spiritually discerned. Which begs the next question, "OK, so how do you do that?"

> These things we also speak, not in words which man's wisdom teaches but which the Holy Spirit teaches, comparing spiritual things with spiritual. But the natural man does not receive the things of the Spirit of God, for they are foolishness to him; nor can he know them, because they are spiritually discerned.
>> —1 Corinthians 2:13–14

THE CAUSE TO PAUSE

When you have reached the end of yourself and you have done all you can do to come clean before God and still feel filthy, it is the cause to pause. Pause. Don't move right or left. Focus on that darkness adjective that you cannot shake for a moment. Don't go one more step until you get alone with God, look Him in the eye, and talk to Him about that emotion, that frustration, that anger problem. Ask Him. Better yet, allow Him to take you to the root. Give Him permission to go anywhere it might lead. Let Him show you the root, because there surely is a root. Here is a real possibility.

Don't be surprised if the person you find in the search for your root is God Himself.

There are many Christians who consciously serve and love God, but way down deep beneath the surface something happened years or months ago that there is no earthly explanation for—other than (in their own minds) a God who could have prevented it, a God who let it happen.

I was walking through this principle several months ago with one of my students. He was a rough, tough, "never-supposed-to-cry" cop who on the outside was the nicest, most easygoing guy you could ever meet, but down deep, he was on a slow burn. He thought he had it all under control and that nobody would notice, but week by week his relationships were eroding and his faith was waning. Week by week, temptation became stronger and stronger, until one day when his wife of only a few years was on the verge of leaving him. She was fed up with him and struggling to keep it together for herself.

When I talked about this root stuff, and especially the part that says that many people find God Himself at the end of their search for a root, something went off in him, and he broke. He and his young wife had experienced a stillbirth just months before, and though he had tried every earthly thing he was supposed to do, he could not find peace. Instead, he became more and more miserable, lonely, angry, and depressed. At first, right after the tragic loss of his baby boy, he attended church every time the doors were open. Only now he was attending alone, and not long after that, he was there less and less. So, when he heard that it was possible that God was the very person he was really angry with, it all made sense. Anger was replaced with confusion and rage with guilt. "How can I be mad at God? What is wrong with me?"

We spoke after class, and he told me, "God could have prevented it, and He didn't. Why? Why did He have to do that? This was our first child together. We looked forward to this. We loved this baby so much, and now he is gone. God just took him, and for what? Why? Why?" And with that, in those few moments of total, raw honesty, that young man began down the road to freedom and release just by being honest and transparent with his God to his God's face. No more pretending. He was like David when he cried out many times, "Where are You, God?"

For the first time, he courageously asked his heart's greatest question, and for the first time, the Lord could begin to answer his questions, comfort him (the Holy Spirit is also called the Comforter), and build him back up.

Does this all sound like spiritual mumbo jumbo? Well then, why do over 80 percent of all marriages that suffer the death of a child end in divorce? Why? You tell me. Because in our rush to move people back into the flow of life, we neglect the ministry of open, honest, full transparency in exchange for pseudoclosure and putting on our best face. Meanwhile, we die inside a little each day.

What do you do if this is you? Get alone with Him today, in the quietness and stillness of your prayer place, and lay those emotions at His feet. Call them out by name, and then just be honest. Allow Him to show you the roots or how to at least begin the process. Give Him permission and the key to the secret places. Don't rush it, but don't be surprised if He brings it to your mind immediately, either. Don't ask amiss. Ask expecting to get an answer. Then, when He shows you and after you have faced it, ask your questions. Allow yourself to go through any grieving, mending, or restoring process that is required, and have your own monkey cage experience. Let it go, never to let it control you again. This is God's way. This is the path He has chosen for you.

> Have I not commanded you? Be strong and courageous. Do not be terrified; do not be discouraged, for the LORD your God will be with you wherever you go.
>
> —Joshua 1:9, NIV

Lastly, find a friend, pastor, or counselor and tell them your story. Allow them a window to your process, and allow them to spark life into your present condition. Above all, remember this: you heard it here first. Don't be surprised to find somewhere down the road that your greatest trial not only becomes your greatest victory, but it also becomes the very testimony that sets others free.

SECTION 3

WILDERNESS CHRISTIANITY

Until I come, devote yourself to the public reading of Scripture, to
preaching and to teaching.... Be diligent in these matters; give yourself
wholly to them, so that everyone may see your progress. Watch your life
and doctrine closely. Persevere in them, because if you do, you will save
both yourself and your hearers.

—1 Timothy 4:13, 15–16, NIV

chapter 10

WILDERNESS CHRISTIANITY 1: LOVE THE LORD WITH ALL YOUR MIND

> But be doers of the word, and not hearers only, deceiving yourselves. For if anyone is a hearer of the word and not a doer, he is like a man observing his natural face in a mirror; for he observes himself, goes away, and immediately forgets what kind of man he was. But he who looks into the perfect law of liberty and continues in it, and is not a forgetful hearer but a doer of the work, this one will be blessed in what he does. If anyone among you thinks he is religious, and does not bridle his tongue but deceives his own heart, this one's religion is useless.
>
> —James 1:22–26

THESE NEXT TWO CHAPTERS WILL BE, BY FAR, TWO OF THE MOST important chapters I have ever written on any topic. What I am about to say to you in these few pages is so incredibly important to the cause of Christ, I believe, that it requires your undivided attention and uninterrupted time. If every reader ever to read this book would grasp and take hold of what I am about to share and then walk it out in their daily life, it would transform the Christian movement in this nation and set about a course of action that would revolutionize the church and the world. Strong words? Yes, but I believe with all my heart that this comes straight from the throne of God.

The church in the United States sits atop a fulcrum, teetering between going on to great things with God or settling for a weekly dose of good news and a handshake. Problem is, to *not* go on with God makes for a church that is a thousand miles wide and only one inch deep. To go on with God means to break through the self-made boundaries of experience and feelings and could hold incredible implications for the multitudes in the valley of decision.

Many in the older generation have concerns about the twenty-first-century church that I believe are worthy of examination and careful consideration. As I examine and consider both, I find that their concerns, and mine as well, are couched in the following statements:

- Controversial statement 1: It is absolutely possible to love God with all of your heart, even to serve Him regularly, and not have His mind on many of the most critical issues of our day. To not have His mind on the issues of the day, secular and spiritual, places the church in a precarious position both inside and outside the walls of the church.

- Controversial statement 2: One of the greatest obstacles to spiritual growth and being a Christian who "walks in the truth" could very well be what many of us love the most— powerful praise and worship. The fear is that we have come to worship the worship experience, feeling that the experience in and of itself is all we need for our walk.

- Controversial statement 3: Incredible services, events, and even powerful preaching become increasingly irrelevant if they do not produce humility, brokenness, hope, and life change— spiritual fruit. The real test of the effectiveness of a church should be the impact that it has on the lives of the individual believer, the community it is in, and the world it seeks to win.

Now, I could think of a few more, but I will surmise that I have at least caused you to want to read on and have piqued your curiosity. So read on you must. I have titled this chapter "Wilderness Christianity" because that is where I believe the vast majority of the church in the United States sits right now, more content with forty years in the wilderness than going forward and having to know God, trust God, and obey God. They are more content with having

Moses go up the mountain to meet with God and then come back and give a report on the meeting so they can continue with their daily routine.

In the chapters ahead, I will continue to make the case for the hour we are in, both as it relates to God's judgment based on our societal situation, and God's timetable based on God's prophetic Word. This teetering between all God has versus all we want to do is the extremely fickle balancing act the church finds itself in. A gentle nudge in the form of a swift kick to the backside away from complacency, apathy, and self-centered pursuits is desperately needed. The momentum so desperately needed at this hour is the simple work of transformation and being transformed. How? In our minds and in our thinking. "Let God transform you inwardly *by a complete change of your mind.* Then you will be able to know the will of God—what is good and is pleasing to him and is perfect" (Rom. 12:2, GNT, emphasis added).

Central to this issue is the paradigm shift of the twenty-first-century church, and especially the megachurch movement, to such a strong emphasis on the Sunday morning experience. Many times this experience comes at the expense of the educational and discipleship programs that were once hallmarks of the evangelical church. The Sunday morning service—and even special events and conferences—can absolutely provide the inspiration and the motivation that can bring a person to a point of decision, even action, and therefore has incredible value in the life of the believer and the life of the church. As an educational model, it falls far short of building the foundational truths into the life of a Christian. It just does.

The praise and worship experience also has incredible potential to create an encounter with the living God, but it can also create an environment where a person can experience a myriad of emotions and feelings in a vacuum, and they leave feeling complete or full of God, as if they have all they need, when, in fact, the strength, courage, and wisdom they will need for everyday life are not housed in the worship experience alone. They just aren't.

So where does that leave you, and what implications does this have for your personal walk with Christ? Well, it means that it does not matter how you feel every week when you leave church, no matter how powerful the preaching or how incredible the praise and worship. The stuff of life happens in the Monday-through-Saturday part of your week, and for that, you will need more. You simply must begin to add more truth to the truth you already have and commit to growing in your faith and in your knowledge and understanding of the Word of God. To do anything less will result in spiritual starvation and a life ruled by the confines of your mortal mind, despite that "full-belly" feeling you have every Sunday when you leave church.

Before I address the concern statements, I need to set the stage, and I know of no better way to start than by telling you about a trip I took to Colorado about twelve years ago with a group of high school seniors. It was August of 1993 when I was a high school principal at a Christian school in the high desert of Southern California. I had signed our seniors up for a leadership summit in the Colorado Springs area and decided to go along with the group to spend time with these awesome kids one last time before they graduated.

We were there for ten full days of intense classes and training, and it was an incredible time for the kids, but for me, there was a lot of down time as I was not a conference teacher or speaker. So I decided to venture out a bit to visit the sights and sounds of the Denver area. During this time, there was one news event that completely dominated everything in all of the local and national news. The pope had come to Denver for the World Youth Festival. It turned out this was one of those "once-in-a-great-many-years" kind of events, and over five hundred thousand Catholics, mostly teens, were scheduled to attend the week's events from all over the world. Five hundred thousand is an amazing number that would catch any eye.

Not being Catholic, I followed the week's events a bit halfheartedly, but it was hard not to stay up with it as it dominated all of the news outlets. I became more keenly interested, though, as the focus of the articles began to really challenge the pope regarding many of the church's conservative stances on social issues. I read article after article where the pope stood his ground and surprisingly received wild applause and approval of the thousands and thousands of teen attendees.

On the last two days of the weeklong event, there was to be a pilgrimage from Mile High Stadium in Denver to a huge vacant field in Cherry Creek,

Colorado, approximately a ten-mile trek to this field where the week would end with a huge Mass on that Friday night followed by another the next morning. It was being billed as a historical event and being tabbed "The Catholic Woodstock."

Boredom and curiosity got the best of me, so I went down, parked my car, and joined the last couple of miles of the pilgrimage and even had a group of priests I befriended sneak me into this massive field that had been fenced off for safety and security measures. I just wanted to be able to say I was there as over five hundred thousand people were expected to attend—and they did not disappoint.

That first night was incredible with all the pageantry as the field filled and the Mass was held. All the passion of thousands of teens assembled gave the evening a college pep rally–type atmosphere right up to the time the pope flew away in the military helicopter. That night there was singing and dancing all night long by teams from all over the world as people waited for the final morning and final Mass of this incredible event.

The next morning came, and the Mass went off about an hour late but with incredible pomp and circumstance. Thousands were fully engrossed in the events of the Mass that August morning. What happened next, though, would shake me to my core and build in me a memory I will never forget. When the Mass was about half-over, the temperature had risen to approximately ninety degrees. That, combined with the altitude, made for conditions that produced a near tragedy that morning in Cherry Creek. One by one, teens all over the place started dropping like flies. They were passing out! I spent the next two hours scooping up teens and adults, carrying them to overrun medical tents. The National Guard was called in as the Mass ended. The toll of people suffering from serious levels of heat exhaustion had reached well over ten thousand. Some even experienced heat stroke and cardiac arrest.

I remember making it back to my car, just spent—emotionally and physically, wondering what just happened back there in that field. Over the course of the next few days, I watched intently to see what the news outlets would say about this tragic course of events. They covered it in great detail. The official number was over fourteen thousand that had been overcome that morning at the Mass.[1]

By far, the most interesting fact that came out of all of this was what the experts determined to be the main cause for the medical emergency. The main cause was dehydration. Now, that may sound obvious to you, and you may think this is not all that profound a conclusion, but the reason for the dehydration is extremely profound and sets the stage for everything else I am going to talk about in this chapter. The reason that so many teens were overcome was because of their diet that week. They had spent the week eating a diet that consisted mostly of candy, soda, and junk food. So here is the kicker: while they did not feel hungry and never felt thirsty, the food they chose to eat and the liquid they consumed in large quantities simply would not and could not sustain life.

This is the exact same thing that happened, in the spirit realm, to the couples mentioned in chapter 4. They chose a spiritual diet that left them feeling full, when in reality they were spiritually empty. OK, here's where we dive in and tackle the controversial statements. For starters, let me lay this groundwork as a starting point. How you "feel" in an incredible church service may be completely inconsequential to your effectiveness, your standing before God, and your spiritual health.

Recently, at my home church we had the incredible honor of hosting Ray McCauley, who is the pastor of a church with approximately forty-eight thousand members in South Africa. Ray met with our staff one morning while he was here. He said a great many things that were very powerful, but one thing he said about the evangelical church in South Africa twenty years ago stuck with me the most. He said, "They [the church members] would go to church racist, have incredible Holy Ghost services, sing their praises, pray their prayers, and have great services, but when they walked out the door, they were still racist." How can this be?

If you can attend a service, experience incredible praise and worship and a powerful message, and weep during the altar call yet go out and continue living with your boyfriend, your faith is of no effect. If you can do the "church thing" and walk out and beat your wife, it is of no effect. If you can attend faithfully every week, go out, and knowingly cheat on your income taxes, it is of no effect. Like the couples in the stories, how they "felt" week to week, in the end, was no more than the rush of candy, soda, and junk food. It could not sustain life. Far too many in the United States evangelical church are living on a diet that will not sustain life much longer if something the size of a revolution does not take place—and soon.

Did you know that every day in America:

- Four children are killed by abuse or neglect?
- Five children or teens commit suicide (that's over eighteen hundred per year)?
- One hundred eighty children are arrested for violent crimes?
- Three hundred eighty are arrested for drug abuse?
- Over eleven hundred babies are born to teenage mothers?
- Over twenty-seven hundred high school students drop out?
- Almost thirty-nine hundred babies are born to unmarried mothers?[2]

As advanced as the war is on a physical and emotional level here in America, the so-called "Christian nation," the war is, believe it or not, just as advanced on a spiritual level with equally devastating eternal implications. The statistics I am about to show you on religion in the new millennium give evidence to this concern.

The statistics are from a research study conducted by George Barna titled "Spiritual Progress Hard to Find in 2003."[3] The article details the findings of his study analyzing more than ten thousand personal interviews nationwide. Barna notes that contradictions and confusion permeate the spiritual condition of the nation. This is huge! Some notable findings of the study are as follows:

- Those who say their religious faith is very important in their own life—84 percent
- Those who claim that their own religious faith is consistently growing deeper—70 percent
- Those who claim to be Christians—84 percent

- Those who say they believe the Bible is totally accurate in all that it teaches—60 percent
- Those who say they are absolutely or somewhat committed to Christianity—75 percent

But the same people said that the following behaviors and lifestyles are "morally acceptable":

- Cohabitation—60 percent
- Gambling—61 percent
- Adultery—42 percent
- Sexual relations between homosexuals—30 percent
- Abortion—45 percent (In the USA, nearly 45 million babies have been sacrificed since the *Roe v. Wade* decision in 1973.)
- Pornography—38 percent
- Use of profanity—36 percent

How can this be? How can a person stand with hands raised to God, weeping and crying out to Him in love and worship, yet walk out thinking and behaving just like the world? Simply put, any decision to follow Christ does not supernaturally impart the wisdom found in God's Word. That takes work. Too many of us want the relationship without doing the things that make for a healthy relationship. Am I suggesting a salvation based on works? Of course not, but I am saying that any good relationship takes work—it just does.

Matthew gives one of the greatest admonitions in Scripture when it says, "'Love the Lord your God with all your heart and with all your soul and with all your mind.' This is the first and greatest commandment" (Matt. 22:37–38, NIV, emphasis added).

I believe there are sincere Christians in the church today who truly love the Lord their God with all of their hearts and with all of their souls but not with their minds—some by ignorance (they simply do not know what God says about this or that) and some by willful rebellion (they want to be their own boss). For others, the problem could simply lie at the feet of a church that does not disciple, teach, or mentor the rank-and-file attendee. Far too often, we "service" them with powerful services and send them on their way, feeling better but unchanged in their thinking and in their understanding of God's Word and His ways.

> Churches can function and even prosper numerically for a time without being biblically sound or focused. God removed His presence from the temple as recorded in Ezekiel 10. Even so, temple worship continued on for hundreds of years.[4]
>
> —Richard Ross

Simply put, we had better care what God thinks about the issues of life— right and wrong—because He cares, and He is a just God. Far too many love Him, even worship Him, only as friend, buddy, or comrade, and they do not fear Him as their God and King. We think He is altogether like us, when He is actually altogether *not* like us. Isaiah 55:8–9 says, "'For my thoughts are not your thoughts, nor are your ways My ways,' says the LORD. 'For as the heavens are higher than the earth, so are My ways higher than your ways, and My thoughts than your thoughts'" (emphasis added).

I cannot say it any clearer: the mind of man will never think the thoughts of God without a transformation of the mind. It is in this transformation that two things will be required: (1) surrender of my right to be an independent, self-determining agent; and (2) submission to the authority of God's Word and His will. First Corinthians 3:18–19 says, "Let no one deceive himself. If anyone among you seems to be wise in this age, let him become a fool that he may become wise. For the wisdom of this world is foolishness with God. For it is written, 'He catches the wise in their own craftiness.'"

TRANSFORMATION 101

So how does one begin the transformation process? Simply put, you have to learn what God has to say about everything. How? You have to become familiar with His Word. If you are doing the work of relationship and drawing near daily, you are halfway there. Now you must learn His commands to keep His commands. In fact, it is in keeping these commands that your love is tested:

But why do you call Me "Lord, Lord," and do not do the things which I say?

—Luke 6:46

Be diligent to present yourself approved by God, a worker who does not need to be ashamed, rightly dividing the word of truth.

—2 Timothy 2:15

All scripture is given by inspiration of God, and is profitable for doctrine, for reproof, for correction, for instruction in righteousness, that the man of God may be complete, thoroughly equipped for every good work.

—2 Timothy 3:16–17

Now, that's a lot to think about for today. In the next chapter, I will tackle controversial statements two and three further, but for now, think on that word *transformation*, and begin the hard work of growing, maturing, and developing the mind of Christ for all God is doing on the earth in our generation.

And do not be conformed to this world, but be transformed by the renewing of your mind, that you may prove what is that good and acceptable and perfect will of God.

—Romans 12:2

chapter 11

WILDERNESS CHRISTIANITY 2: HOW WE KNOW THAT WE KNOW HIM

> Now by this we know that we know Him, if we keep His commandments. He who says, "I know Him," and does not keep His commandments, is a liar, and the truth is not in him. But whoever keeps His word, truly the love of God is perfected in him. By this we know that we are in Him. He who says he abides in Him ought himself also to walk just as He walked.
>
> —1 John 2:3–6

WHEN MOSES WENT UP THE MOUNTAIN TO MEET WITH THE God of the universe, life in the valley below had all the markings of a religious people—fellowship, song and dance, and powerful praise and worship. Problem is, the object of their worship was a cow made of gold and not the God who had delivered them, saved them, fed them, clothed them, and protected them.

The power of praise and worship in the church is enormous, but so is the power of music in general. So when one experiences all of the incredible emotions and feelings of a powerful worship song, while standing in the midst of perhaps thousands of others standing and singing along, is it the worship that feels so strong on you, or is it the music? Can a teenager experience incredible worship in church yet walk out and use language that he or she would never use in church? They certainly can if it's just music. Can two unwed lovers experience the depths of love for God, knowing the depth of their sin, and yet feel no conviction of that sin and continue in it week after week? They can with powerful music.

How could a person feel so right yet be so far outside God's will for their lives? How could this occur? One of the most revered men of God that I know tells the story of counseling a young couple from his church several years ago who were engaged to be married. They both came to him wanting him to marry them, only to have their pastor painfully tell them that he simply could not perform their wedding ceremony in good conscience, knowing that the couple had been living together for several months.

This shocked the young couple considerably, but it rocked the pastor even more. How could a couple who faithfully attended his church and sat under his teaching for so long not have any compulsion or conviction for doing something so contrary to God's Word? The young couple explained that they would go to his church faithfully every week, raise their hands in worship, and truly love the Lord, then go home from church and have sex.

In the end, they came back to the pastor and repented, seeing in Scripture and through his counsel that what they had done was wrong. He challenged them to live apart for one year and then consider marriage. They did, and one year later he married them. They are still rockin' on today!

IN SPIRIT AND IN TRUTH

To love God only with all your heart and all your soul is incomplete and is missing one of the most important factors of becoming like Christ—your mind. Scripture makes it abundantly clear: don't say you love Him and then not keep His commands. He says, "What is love?" Then He answers, "To keep My commandments." To know God's mind means that you must take the next major step into the next level—and in my opinion, it is the most important step. You must come under the authority of God's Word, the Holy Bible. You cannot have God's mind on the things of this life apart from allowing that mind to teach you His Word through the power of the Holy Spirit.

So what's my point? Well, let's take a look at the controversial statements two and three:

- Controversial statement 2: One of the greatest obstacles to spiritual growth and being a Christian who "walks in the truth" may very well be what many of us love the most—powerful praise and worship.

- Controversial statement 3: Incredible services, events, and even powerful preaching become completely irrelevant if they do not produce humility, brokenness, hope, and life change—spiritual fruit.

Wow! That's a powerfully strong accusation to make. I better be able to back it up because this one can get a man beat up in the church parking lot. How critical to the church experience is worship in the twenty-first century? It is enormously important. So let's take a look and unpack it for a moment.

The bottom line is that music, religious or otherwise, makes us feel a lot of things—happy, joyful, sad, reflective, in love, playful, and even contemplative—but the church experience, including the praise and worship portion of the service, should do more—*will* do more. True worship is to worship in spirit and in truth. Singer/songwriter Chris Tomlin said, "True worship is not just the words and the music. True worship is about changing people's lives."[1]

> Worship anticipates not only an encounter with God, but also a clear next word from God. Worship is totally God centered! God focused! Out of worship comes a clearer and more focused relationship of faith and obedience with God. Worship is God's way of developing character and directing the life into the center of His will. *The ultimate outcome of consistent worship is a life totally yielded to God, on God's terms.*[2]
> —Henry Blackaby, emphasis added

The Old Testament Book of Amos is an incredible book of prophecy written at a time when the children of Israel were rebelling against God. In this book, God was absolutely fed up, especially critical, and outright disgusted with His people, the children of Israel. He had *had* it! And soon they would experience His judgment as never before. Throughout the last half of the Book of Amos, and especially in chapter 5, we find something very interesting about God's chosen people that, I believe, parallels with the evangelical church in the twenty-first century. Chapter 5 states in verses 21–24: "I hate, I despise your feast days, and I do not savor your sacred assemblies. Though you offer Me burnt offerings and your grain offerings, I will not accept them, nor will I regard your fattened peace offerings. Take away from me the noise of your songs, for I will not hear the melody of your stringed instruments. But let justice run down like water, and righteousness like a mighty stream."

Then, a little further down in chapter 6, God continues:

> Woe to you who put far off the day of doom,
> Who cause the seat of violence to come near;
> Who lie on beds of ivory,
> Stretch out on your couches,
> Eat lambs from the flock
> And calves from the midst of the stall;
> Who sing idly to the sound of stringed instruments,
> And invent for yourselves musical instruments like David;
> Who drink wine from bowls,
> And anoint yourselves with the best ointments,
> *But are not grieved for the affliction of Joseph.*
> Therefore they shall now go captive as the first of the captives,
> And those who recline at banquets shall be removed.
> —Amos 6:3–7, emphasis added

OK, so what does this have to do with worship? Well, it isn't so much a worship issue as it is a spiritual ignorance issue in a desensitized church. Here are a few facts about the people of Israel, Zion, and Samaria in the scriptures above.

The most important thing to note is that these folks were thick in sin—walking in it, living in it, and committing acts daily that grieved their heavenly Father. All the while, they commemorated all of the holy days. They assembled in sacred assemblies weekly (church), experienced music services in songs they offered up to God (praise and worship), and gave faithfully to the church (tithes and offerings). They went about their daily lives as though they were completely unaware of an angry God and the stench of their daily sin. The Book of Psalms says it like this:

> But to the wicked God says:
> "What right have you to declare My statutes,
> Or take My covenant in your mouth,
> Seeing you hate instruction
> And cast My words behind you?
> When you saw a thief, you consented with him,
> And have been a partaker with adulterers.
> You give your mouth to evil,
> And your tongue frames deceit.
> You sit and speak against your brother;
> You slander your own mother's son.
> These things you have done, and I kept silent;
> *You thought that I was altogether like you;*
> But I will rebuke you,
> And set them in order before your eyes.
>
> Now consider this, you who forget God,
> Lest I tear you in pieces,
> And there be none to deliver:
> *Whoever offers praise glorifies Me;*
> *And to him who orders his conduct aright*
> I will show the salvation of God."
> —Psalm 50:16–23, emphasis added

In other words, God's judgment, thankfully, is tempered with His mercy. He sees your life—all of it—and He implores you to consider your ways. This powerful verse makes every effort to tell you that all of your church stuff is completely null and void, a waste of time, and that dirty hands lifted to Him are not emblems of praise; they're just dirty hands. He calls you and me to pure worship with conduct aright and a life lived under the authority of His Word. In Luke, Jesus asked this simple question: "Why do you call Me 'Lord, Lord' and do not do the things which I say?" (Luke 6:46).

Music—secular or sacred—is a powerful medium. Add to that the full instrumentation of a large church and you have a powerful, professional sound, and with that, enormous power over emotions and even the thoughts of a man or woman. A trip to any big-name secular concert will prove that. The power that comes through true praise and worship, in context with the full counsel of God, is an incredibly powerful tool for teaching and experiencing the presence of God. The feelings associated with music are universal and, I believe, very similar to the effects of an excellent worship set.

> What is worship? What are we doing when we worship? True worship is when your spirit adores and connects with the Spirit of God. When the very core of your being is found in loving Him…lost in Him. The essence of worship is when our heart and soul, all that is within you, adores and connects with the Spirit of God. *In fact, regardless of how magnificent the musical moments are, unless your heart is fully engaged in the worship being expressed…it is still only music.* The pure song of a heart that is yearning for more of God and less of himself is the music that holds the key to so many victories…and delights the heart of our king.[3]

If you looked at an action-packed secular concert, you would see great similarities to the worship experiences of most churches. The difference must be in the actual manifest presence of a living God. Jack Hayford said, "Worship is the key to evangelism, but true worship comes through access, and some songs do not allow access. Some worship leaders' presentations do not allow access—it only allows onlookers." That is why the praise and worship experience in a church must not be held in a vacuum and instead must be examined in direct association with the lives of the worshipers, and especially the worship leaders. Otherwise, we send people out of our services with a myriad of emotions, which can be incredibly revealing or tragically deceptive.

> Those who live according to the flesh set their minds on the things of the flesh, but those who live according to the Spirit, the things of the Spirit.... So then, those who are in the flesh cannot please God.
> —Romans 8:5, 8

This is why Scripture so strongly admonishes pastors, teachers, and worship pastors/leaders concerning their responsibility, at the pulpit and from the stage, to spread not only love and hope but also truth and the full counsel of Scripture. Otherwise one can walk into a church a sinner, experience all of the right "feelings," and walk out only to continue in his sin, feeling like he has been with God and that all is well.

> I charge you therefore before God and the Lord Jesus Christ, who will judge the living and the dead at His appearing and His kingdom: Preach the word! Be ready in season and out of season. Convince, rebuke, exhort, with all longsuffering and teaching. For the time will come when they will not endure sound doctrine, but according to their own desires, because they have itching ears, they will heap up for themselves teachers; and they will turn their ears away from the truth, and be turned aside to fables. But you be watchful in all things, endure afflictions, do the work of an evangelist, fulfill your ministry.
> —2 Timothy 4:1–5

I have personally witnessed in many churches entire choirs, frontline singers, and musicians give everything they have, even weep during a powerful praise and worship set, and then walk off the stage prior to the message and have coffee and fellowship until the service is over. Now, I realize that many churches have multiple services and that it is common to fellowship during the down time, but I don't know what to think about not attending the preaching or teaching time of any service at all. I give this word of admonishment: we have to be so careful in our worship communities that we do not allow ourselves to worship our worship or the praise and worship service itself.

These are very strong words for leaders and anybody who stands on the platform representing Christ to the people today. People absolutely need an encounter with the living God, but an encounter is not the only goal. The goal is for a changed life, a word in season, repentance, mercy, even salvation. That goal will not be realized in the life of the person in the pew if it is not lived out in the life of every man and woman who dare to stand on that platform—frontline and choir especially. We live in an age when the church is in great danger. Shallow faith won't sustain the heat of the day and the comings and goings of a world walking through trials daily. Lives are at stake, families are at stake, and our God is watching.

That leads us back to you, the reader of this book. It is entirely possible for you to go to church and *feel* really good, or really sad, or really inspired, or really emotional, or really anything and still not know God. It is also possible to give your offerings, serve in a ministry, and never miss a service, and not have God's mind on the circumstances in your life and in the decisions you are making. In the words of Ray McCauley of the South African church during apartheid, if you can walk into a service a racist, *feel* all of those feelings in a Holy Ghost meeting, and walk out a racist, you are no more connected to your Savior than someone who never walked through the doors of the church—only it's worse: you are without excuse. Add your own metaphor for "racist," and complete your own sentence. The end result is the same.

> Not everyone who says to Me, "Lord, Lord," shall enter the kingdom of heaven, but he who does the will of My Father in heaven. Many will say to Me in that day, "Lord. Lord, have we not prophesied in Your name, cast out demons in Your name, and done many wonders in Your name?" And then I will declare to them, "I never knew you; depart from Me, you who practice lawlessness."
>
> —Matthew 7:21–23

You stand today at a place I refer to as the tipping point. It is the place where you can decide to stay right where you are, content with holy ignorance and hoping for the best, but you will stand there thinking your own thoughts and doing what your own thoughts reason is best. Or you can surrender your right to yourself, bow your knee, and come under the authority of God's Word, whatever that might mean and wherever that might lead.

We are commanded to worship. Praise God for worship that can usher us into the very presence of God, but we must worship in spirit *and* in truth and allow God to speak in that powerful time *to* you *about* you.

> Whenever we realize that we have not done that which we had magnificent opportunity of doing, then we are apt to sink into despair; and Jesus comes and says, "Sleep on now, that opportunity is lost forever, you cannot alter it, but arise and go to the next thing." Let the past sleep, but let it sleep on the bosom of Christ, and go out into the irresistible future with Him. If we are inspired by God, what is the next thing? To trust Him absolutely and to pray on the ground of His Redemption. Never let the sense of failure corrupt your new action.[4]
>
> —Oswald Chambers

SECTION 4

COME UNDER AUTHORITY

SECULAR WISDOM—EXISTENTIALISM

A philosophical attitude that stresses the individual's unique position as a self-determining agent, responsible for the authenticity of his or her own choices and experiences *absent the existence of a higher authority.*

—Man

GODLY WISDOM—LORDSHIP

He who has My commandments and keeps them, it is he who loves Me. And he who loves Me will be loved by My Father, and I will love him and manifest Myself to him.

—Jesus (John 14:21)

chapter 12

Battleground Earth

> Finally, my brethren, be strong in the Lord and in the power of His might. Put on the whole armor of God, that you may be able to stand against the wiles of the devil. For we do not wrestle against flesh and blood, but against principalities, against powers, against the rulers of the darkness of this age, against spiritual hosts of wickedness in the heavenly places. Therefore take up the whole armor of God, that you may be able to withstand in the evil day, and having done all, to stand.
>
> —Ephesians 6:10–13

IN OUR QUEST TO LIVE LIFE AT THE NEXT LEVEL, IT IS CRITICAL TO realize the most important focus in the battle—the prize. The prize Satan seeks to have is the souls of men and women. The second most important thing to realize in this battle is the strategy for victory. The strategy Satan has employed in the last forty-plus years has been an all-out offensive, seeking to take precious strategic ground. That ground is:

1.   The mind of man
2.   The children of man

Throughout the Middle Ages—those dark days of the church—the strategy of Satan was to destroy and rid our faith in the Word of God. Throughout the Crusades and the Inquisitions and under the rule of many corrupt and ungodly kings and queens, many martyrs were tortured, banished, or burned at the stake simply because they would not relinquish or renounce the truths written by God in the Holy Scriptures. That plan failed, as the blood of the martyrs served only to strengthen the movement—a lesson Satan should have learned at the cross.

Prior to that, Satan's plan was simply to keep the Word of God in the hands of corrupt priests and in languages the common churchgoer could not understand. This actually worked for a season, but then God raised up an individual named Martin Luther who took a courageous stand, and with that one act of bravery, the Reformation was born. With the stroke of that same man's brave hand, and others such as Wycliffe, the Bible was translated into other languages. Then, Johannes Gutenberg invented something called the printing press—and *voilà*! The world would never be the same as the Word of God was liberated and began to saturate the countryside—the same countrysides where the blood of the martyrs once ran down.

Prior to that, Satan committed the ultimate offense and tried to silence the faith with the most horrific emblem of execution known in that time, or in any time to follow—the cross. On that cross, all seemed lost for the Christian faithful, and Satan thought he had defeated the very God of the universe, but just as he would be throughout the ages—he was wrong. It turned out that he did not know the God of Abraham, David, and Jesus half as much as he thought he did. When Christ arose on the third day, it was finished. All that was left for Satan at that point was a race to the finish line with a goal of taking as many with him to an eternity in hell as he possibly could.

Problem is, while he did not know our God and while he did not factor in the Resurrection, he does know the mind of man and the flesh that man is housed in. By virtue of the Fall and his own experience and nature, he knows all too well our strong desire to be the boss of our own lives and the masters of our own fate. He also knows about the longing of our heart for a relationship with our Creator and that the longing of our flesh can sometimes drown out the desire of our heart. He knows that all he needs to do is keep us from the desire of our heart and fill our minds with the things of the flesh. Thus our disastrous flirtation as a nation with drugs, alcohol, fornication, material wealth, abortion, homosexuality, and corruption.

Another important truth that Satan has learned through the centuries is that full-out frontal assaults don't always work, especially for the current generation and for the generations to follow. He has learned that patience plus distraction plus pleasure produce an existence that makes us completely unaware of the forces that have infiltrated and that are now among us. It's like the sneak attack of guerrilla warfare. In civilian clothes, they claim just enough lives day after day to stay under the radar of our collective Christian consciousness. Bigger problem is, he can no longer afford to be patient. The attack that is about to happen will be of much greater magnitude, on a much grander scale, against a much weaker, unprepared church unless we awaken, realize that the play is over, and turn our focus to the activity of the kingdom.

THE CHILDREN OF MAN

Satan has learned that there are places where Christians are not present in any sizeable numbers and that in those places incredible gains can be made. Worse yet, he has learned from thousands of years of history that if you can turn the heart of just one generation, you can win the war. This is where our absence from public discourse has hurt us the most. The most substantial gains for evil have come in the places where our children live and learn. We slept through a forty-year period of time that saw the following take place:

- Prayer in schools—rejected
- The Ten Commandments displayed—rejected
- Presence of a Creator in science—rejected
- Creationism as a truth—rejected
- Creationism as a theory—rejected
- Corporal punishment—banished
- The Virgin Birth—impossible
- A resurrection from the dead—improbable
- Christmas vacation—rejected
- Easter vacation—rejected
- Christian prayer at graduation—rejected
- Christ mentioned in graduation speeches—rejected
- Sanctity of life—rejected
- Right and wrong—relative

- A parent's right to know if their child is going to have an abortion—rejected
- Abstinence—rejected
- Influence of Christian Scripture, principles, and men in the founding documents of this country—retracted

We slept while the enemy marched on some of our most treasured ground, and that ground is now a fortress, held by an enemy that never sleeps. His recipe for success was to simply sit by and let man be man. Sooner or later he knew our selfish pride and our longing to live the American Dream would cause us to abandon those hallowed halls that made those dreams come true decades ago, in pursuit of affluence and leisure.

DECEPTIVELY WEAK

Here is the biggest problem of all as I see it: we think we are much stronger individually than we really are. Problem is, we are only as strong collectively as we are individually.

One of my favorite movies is *The Last Samurai*, starring Tom Cruise. Now, I am not the greatest Tom Cruise fan, but my wife certainly is. So when a new Tom Cruise movie comes out, we are typically there to see it during the first week it opens.

There is a scene in *The Last Samurai* that I think is incredibly symbolic of where many of us in the church are today. In this particular scene, Tom Cruise walks out to face his adversary for a training session. Tom is bigger than his adversary, much cooler dressed than his adversary, and carries a weapon of equal size and capable of as much power as his opponents weapon.

The scene is so dramatic as our hero, Tom Cruise, steps up. All eyes of the village are watching. He glares unafraid into the eyes of his opponent. Then he takes his stance, lifts his weapon, and prepares for an all-out assault on his much smaller and weaker opponent. Then it happens—*biff, boom, bam!* Three swift smacks from his opponent's weapon and Tom Cruise is lying facedown in the mud, humiliated and stinging from the blows of the stick, but he's Tom Cruise, so he gets up, strikes an even stronger pose, and readies himself, and then it's on once again. This time there are five swift blows in succession, and our hero is once again facedown in the mud, more battered and humiliated than before.

This is the story for many of us. We look physically able and competent. We are willing. We look like good Christians. We mean well, give faithfully, and serve where needed, but spiritually, the vast majority of us do not possess or know how to use the armor of faith properly. If we could look at our spirit man, we would look like emaciated, undernourished, and starving, with our hands up, declaring, "Here am I, Lord. Send me."

This scenario with Tom Cruise repeats itself three or four more times before he is lain facedown in the mud, completely beaten to a pulp and defeated by a much smaller, weaker opponent with the entire village looking on. I watched this on the big screen and thought to myself, "That's us. That's what's happening to the church." For the first time in a long time, there are more churches shutting their doors in our country than there are new ones opening. The population is growing at a very rapid rate, and the church is not keeping pace. There are more megachurches in this country today than at any other point in history, yet every damning social statistic is as high as it has ever been.

Somehow, we have to become salt and light again. We have to commit to the hard work of spiritual growth—maturity—to grow into the mighty army we were made to be. Christianity is not merely a philosophy; it is a way of living that demands our focus, our time, and our very lives. What we need is a full transformation in our thinking, not new thinking, but a commitment to knowing and doing the will of God. Good news is, we have the manual. Better news is, you are as close to God as you want to be.

> It was he who gave some to be apostles, some to be prophets, some to be evangelists, and some to be pastors and teachers, to prepare God's people for works of service, *so that the body of Christ may be built up* until we all reach unity in the faith and in the knowledge of the Son of God and *become mature*, attaining to the whole measure of the fullness of Christ.

Then we will no longer be infants, *tossed back and forth by the waves, and blown here and there by every wind of teaching and by the cunning and craftiness of men in their deceitful scheming.* Instead, *speaking the truth in love,* we will in all things grow up into him who is the Head, that is, Christ. *From him the whole body, joined and held together by every supporting ligament, grows and builds itself up in love, as each part does its work.*

—Ephesians 4:11–16, NIV, emphasis added

chapter 13

BUILDING YOUR SPIRITUAL HOUSE

Blessed is the man
>who does not walk in the counsel of the wicked
or stand in the way of sinners
>or sit in the seat of mockers.
But his delight is in the law of the LORD,
>and on his law he meditates day and night.
He is like a tree planted by streams of water,
>which yields its fruit in season
and whose leaf does not wither.
>Whatever he does prospers.
>
>—Psalm 1:1–3, NIV

THE APOSTLE PAUL IS THE PERFECT EXAMPLE FOR THE WHOLE "come-under-authority" concept. There he was, just walking along on his way to persecute another bunch of those Christ followers when—*shazam!*—a bright light blinded him, and everything went blurry. God is on the scene in a big way, and suddenly, Paul (named Saul at the time) is confronted with a choice: will he bend his knee to the God of the universe—a new truth for Paul—or will he reject God and hold to his strongly held belief system? He was challenged to come under the authority of the living God—just like you. Do you think it was an easy decision? Think again.

Allow me to go deeper for a moment. Over the course of my career, I have developed relationships with a wide variety of people. Many of them do not know Jesus as their personal Savior. Three or four years ago, through my job, I developed a friendship with a young woman who was very different than I was politically, socially, and certainly religiously. This person was, and still is, extremely intelligent, quick-minded, and progressive in her thinking.

She would be what conservative talk radio refers to as a "classic liberal." I just knew her as my dear friend.

While she put up a good front, I was always aware that there was a hurt somewhere in her past, a hurt she would never fully divulge. She also had the blessing and/or curse of being the daughter of a pastor, which I had always felt had something to do with the hurt she so aptly kept under wraps. Over the course of a few years while working together, she and I would have lengthy conversations about everything under the sun, and while we were very different, we also both respected the other greatly and were good friends professionally.

The one thing she would say pretty regularly about us "Christians" had to do with how "narrow-minded" we all were. Finally one day, I stopped her in her tracks, and I asked if I could put her "narrow-minded" theory to the test. She allowed me to do just that. I asked her to think of two of her most deeply held beliefs about any two social issues. After giving her a few minutes to come up with her big two, I then began to put her faith to the challenge. I asked her the following question: "If God, *the* God of the universe, stood before you right now and told you that the two beliefs on social issues that you hold deepest were wrong beliefs, that His views were the opposite, and that He wanted you to change your positions, what would you do? Would you submit and change your view in obedience to Him, or would you have to declare, 'Then You can't be my God'?"

This hit her hard. You see, today's "spiritual person," as it is defined by the dominant philosophy of our culture, is referred to by the philosophical gurus of today as an *existentialist*. Existentialism is defined as "a philosophical attitude that stresses the individual's unique position as a self-determining agent, responsible for the authenticity of his or her own choices and experiences absent the existence of a higher authority." Surrender is simply not part of the lexicon for a true existentialist.

As I watched my friend reflect on the question I posed to her, I could see that she would have to confess that if this were the case, then He could not be her God. She then, like a wounded dog in a fight, challenged me with the same question. I told her that this was my point exactly. She looked puzzled.

I explained that a true Christian forfeits all rights to what he or she thinks or feels about anything and freely gives those rights to our God and His Word. Our goal is to have His mind and to know what He thinks, whether or not we are capable of understanding or agree on a gut level.

I then drove it deeper and told her that to me, for her to have her own beliefs, beliefs that not even God could change, was far more "narrow-minded" than the astute Christian who is open to anything that God says is true. I told her that being open to growth and change, for a true follower of Christ, was an every-day-of-every-year experience, because as we go deeper into the Word of God, we are confronted with the reality of all there is that we do not know—yet.

I told her of how drug addicts were set free, marriages were saved, homes were restored, and lives were changed, not because people refused to open their minds, but because they opened their minds to anything and everything their Creator told them. People are not born with the instinct to give, let alone give 10 percent of their income, go to a foreign country to serve others, or give up their Sunday mornings. These disciplines are learned by people with open minds, open hearts, and open arms—quite the opposite of those whose god amazingly has the same views on every subject under the sun as they do. My friend, my precious friend, choked by the cares of this world and her insistence on being the boss of her own life, the master of her own universe, could not get to the place required to cross over from unbelief to belief—surrender.

The Book of Luke paints a great picture of the church in any age and the struggles it goes through in trying to walk in the truth. (See Luke 8:11–15.) The passage speaks of four kinds of people at for different levels of hearing and receiving the Word of God.

1. "By the wayside." These are the ones who hear the word but never believe.

2. "On the rock." Those whose hearts and minds are likened to a rocky surface hear the Word, get all fired up, but fail to sprout a root system and therefore die when the heat hits.

3. "Among thorns." These are those who receive the Word but are so "choked with cares, riches, and pleasures of life" that they are not able to develop or produce fruit.

4. "On good ground." These people represent good, fertile soil and—you guessed it—produce great crops.

I want to focus on the folks in the second and third scenario—those with rocks for brains and those living among the weeds. To draw near to God means so much more than just an experience; it is a relationship. It is a commitment to listening, learning, and growing, not in a vacuum, but rather through the study of God's Word, where you will find His mind on anything and everything you will ever need to know. From there, it is simply a matter of obedience. Ignorance will no longer serve as your defense.

> I will show you what he is like who comes to me and hears my words and puts them into practice. He is like a man building a house, who dug down deep and laid the foundation on rock. When a flood came, the torrent struck that house but could not shake it, because it was well built. But the one who hears my words and does not put them into practice is like a man who built a house on the ground without a foundation. The moment the torrent struck that house, it collapsed and its destruction was complete.
>
> —Luke 6:47–49, NIV

What about you? Think of your most strongly held social value. Pick any one you like. Got it? OK, now, suppose God were to come to you directly and say, "That is not what I think about that topic. I think differently." Now what would you do? Would you immediately say to your God, "Then I now officially change my view to conform to Yours. I may not understand right now, nevertheless, I yield my desire, knowing that Your thoughts are higher than mine." Or would you say, "Then You can't be my God." Which would it be?

BLESS THE LORD

Let's take it a step deeper. How about your future? Are you willing to surrender yourself to whatever God would have you become and wherever He would have you go? I know so many Christians who have it all figured out. They know which ministry they want to serve in, how they want to do it, and where they want to go, but when it doesn't come to fruition, or when it simply does not work the way they planned, they become disillusioned and discouraged. So they try harder, pray harder, and stay after it, only to discover that nothing changes. Soon, discouragement, frustration, and disillusionment set in, and it's not long before we stop seeing these folks around—and that's tragic.

We in the church have to stop doing things for God and then asking Him to bless it. That is so *not* the scriptural model. We have such a limited view of what ministry is, and it is so much broader than we ever imagined. We limit God tremendously in our lives when we tell Him what we intend to do for Him. When we do that, we become that hardened ground, that rocky surface, and roots can't grow deep because we do not let them in for fear they will sprout a plant we do not care to house or tend to. We don't let them lodge in us because they simply do not look anything like the tree we intend to grow.

I have a very close friend who has been in worship ministry pretty much his entire adult life. He is a very talented singer, and everywhere he has gone to church, he has been one of the main singers and soloists. At least that's how it was until he landed at his most recent church. This church already had a full supply of frontline worship singers and soloists, and all they had room for was for him to be one of about one hundred choir members. Well, he jumped in and was faithful in the choir for months, knowing how completely unaware the leaders were of his talent and previous experience.

After two years of singing on the third row, he began to become frustrated and began to think the Lord had passed him by, but with everything in him he could not understand why. He became one of the key leaders in the choir, but never was able to hold that microphone or be on the front line. Wow! This was hard. His problem before this church was always the opposite—too many requests for his time and always being needed on the worship team and for solos. To this precious saint, this was just crazy, but to see what God was doing, you need to hear the rest of the story.

Several years prior, this warrior had lost his first child and had suffered through all of the stages of grief associated with this life-changing experience. He had walked through that storm and had come out on the other side still married, able to have other children, and able to get on with his life, loving God, spiritually healthy, and serving Him—full of hope. During his three years at this new church, several other young couples lost children, and all of a sudden, he found himself in the middle of the very needy, extremely volatile lives of men who now had to walk where he had walked. The head of the counseling program at the church came to him and told him that he was desperately needed to work with these young men either in a special small group or in some kind of support group situation. After giving it some thought, he said no.

Actually, he didn't exactly say no, but instead, he just never really followed through with contacting the other men; he never set anything up, and he never really gave it much thought. After all, this wasn't his ministry. His ministry was worship. He was also a great prayer warrior with many requests to serve in the altar ministry. Again, he politely said no. Again, he believed his ministry was worship and the choir, and that required too much of his time to allow him to add one more commitment.

Henry Blackaby, in his life-changing workbook titled *Experiencing God*, says that some of the most critical principles for knowing and doing the will of God are to allow God to show you where He is working and to consider that when God shows you where He is working, He is inviting you to join Him in that work. We should then go immediately and do it.[1] So how about my friend? Whose agenda was he using?

Coming under authority is not simply coming under another person or spiritual leader; it is so much more than that. To come under authority means to be sensitive to the movement of God in your life (discernment), and then, when you hear Him call you to something, you do it. It simply means doing one of the hardest things there is for carnal man to do—surrender.

Are you open to anything and everything God might have for you to do? Or are you committed to making your dreams come true? Who's the boss of your one life to live?

> And this I pray, that your love may abound still more and more in *knowledge and all discernment*, that you may approve the things that are excellent, that you may be sincere and without offense till the day of Christ, being filled with the fruits of righteousness *which are by Jesus Christ*, to the glory and praise of God.
>
> —Philippians 1:9–11, emphasis added

Are you willing to let God do whatever He wants to do with you today? Are you willing to bow the knee of your own will, your own dreams, and your own desires and take on the mantle He has prepared for you for such a time as this? Paul was, and it changed the course of history. My dear friend at work was not, and she wanders in darkness, confusion, and isolation to this very day. My choir friend is somewhere in between. He is learning day by day to see the hand of God and is now open to the possibility that his plans for himself may not be God's plan. This broken Christian man is learning that he has weaknesses and even blind spots in areas he never thought possible, and he is walking the path of vulnerability and obedience even as we speak. I believe that with every step of obedience he takes, he will find joy unspeakable and a usefulness unlike any he has ever encountered, serving his God in his generation God's way.

chapter 14

DESTINATION TRANSFORMATION

This I say, therefore, and testify in the Lord, that you should no longer walk as the rest of the Gentiles walk, in the futility of their mind, having their understanding darkened, being alienated from the life of God, because of the ignorance that is in them, because of the hardening of their heart; who, being past feeling, have given themselves over to lewdness, to work all uncleanness with greediness. But you have not so learned Christ, if indeed you have heard Him and have been taught by Him, as the truth is in Jesus: that you put off, concerning your former conduct, the old man which grows corrupt according to the deceitful lusts, and be renewed in the spirit of your mind, and that you put on the new man which was created according to God, in true righteousness and holiness.

—Ephesians 4:17–24

TRANSFORMED IS A POWERFUL WORD, BUT WHAT DOES IT MEAN? Rick Warren, in his book *The Purpose Driven Life*, points out an incredibly important fact about the word *transformed*.

The Greek word for transformed is metamorphosis (used in Romans 12:2 and 2 Corinthians 3:18), which is used today to describe the amazing change a caterpillar goes through in becoming a butterfly. It is a beautiful picture of what happens to us spiritually when we allow God to direct our thoughts: We are changed from the inside out, we become more beautiful, and we are set free to soar to new heights.[1]

What I am talking about is an entirely new way of thinking. You see, as pointed out previously in Isaiah, God's ways and His thoughts are so much higher and different from ours. We don't see what He sees, hear what He hears, or feel what He feels, but we can. We absolutely can, and that is what I mean when I say to "come under authority." First Corinthians 2:14–16 says, "But the natural man does not receive the things of the Spirit of God, for they are foolishness to him; nor can he know them, because they are spiritually discerned. But he who is spiritual judges all things, yet he himself is rightly judged by no one. For 'who has known the mind of the LORD that he may instruct Him?' But we have the mind of Christ."

You see, God stands ready to do a work *in* you so that He can do a work *through* you. The lifelong thought process that says that we are to build ourselves up to go do a work for the Lord is a faulty premise. It has never been about us doing work for God. His goal is that our own flesh decreases so that His Spirit might increase and do a work through us. We are just the vessel, but what an awesome thing it is to be that kind of vessel. The Book of John says, "He must increase, but I must decrease.... He who has received His testimony has certified that God is true. For He whom God has sent speaks the words of God, for God does not give the Spirit by measure" (John 3:30, 33–34).

This is John talking about Jesus. Even Jesus speaks only the words God gives Him to say and does nothing of His own accord. Think I am overstating this? Think again as you read the very words of Jesus on this topic: "My Father is always at his work to this very day, and I, too, am working...*I tell you the truth, the Son can do nothing by himself; he can do only what he sees his Father doing*, because whatever the Father does the Son also does. For the Father loves the Son and shows him all he does" (John 5:17, 19–20, NIV, emphasis added).

Also from John: "He will not speak on his own; he will speak only what he hears, and he will tell you what is yet to come" (John 16:13, NIV).

And from the Book of Psalms: "The LORD foils the plans of the nations; he thwarts the purposes of the peoples. But the plans of the LORD stand firm forever, the purposes of his heart through all generations" (Ps. 33:10–11, NIV).

Here's the thing: God doesn't need our plan to save the world. He already has a plan. Our job is to enter into relationship with Him, to begin the process of taking on His mind through the study of His Word, and then to submit to His authority over our lives by surrendering our right to ourselves so that He can do an incredible work through us. This whole process of taking on the mind of Christ is what Scripture refers to as "the renewing of your mind." The Good News Translation of the Bible says it this way: "Let God transform you inwardly by a compete change of your mind. Then you will be able to know the will of God; what is good and is pleasing to him and is perfect" (Rom. 12:2).

> [For my determined purpose is] that I may know Him [that I may progressively become more deeply and intimately acquainted with Him, perceiving and recognizing and understanding the wonders of His Person more strongly and more clearly], and that I may in that same way come to know the power out-flowing from His resurrection [which it exerts over believers]…to be continually transformed [in spirit into His likeness even] to His death.
>
> —Philippians 3:10, AMP

Do you see the scriptural pattern? Are you beginning to understand the need for surrender, study, intimacy, and prayer? It is a lifestyle we are talking about, not a weekly experience or an emotional high. One of the leading authorities in Christian research in the United States, George Barna, made the following astute summation after spending year after year studying trends and attitudes in the American church:

> The reason why Christians are so similar in their attitudes, values, and lifestyles to non-Christians is that they were not sufficiently challenged to *think and behave differently—radically differently* based on core spiritual perspectives when they were children. Simply getting people to go to church regularly is not the key to becoming a mature Christian. *Spiritual transformation requires a more extensive investment in one's ability to interpret all life situations in spiritual terms.*[2]

The battle is for the mind of man and the children of man. Never forget that. God's plan for victory is simply this: that the rank-and-file Christian would so radically alter their focus off of the things of the world and onto the things of the kingdom to see what is really happening in the hour we live in. How? By drawing near in relationship with Christ, allowing Him to do the work of purification in our lives, and then by surrendering all right to ourselves and coming under the authority of God's Holy Word by a renewing of our mind.

The result: a grassroots move of God whereby His people begin to see what He sees, hear what He hears, feel what He feels, and do what He would do, going anywhere He says to go! Praise God! It is so within our reach, and He is so ready to take us there.

A DIVINE APPOINTMENT

It was February 2007, and I was deep into the writing of this book, and even more specifically, this section of the book, when I had to go to Southern California for an appointment. Well, anyone who has ever written a book knows about deadlines. When you are in a flow and every word is flying off the end of your fingertips, you don't want to break that rhythm for anything. It was during this February trip that I found myself in the town I grew up in, Palmdale, California, at my mother's house. My goal was to get three or four days of uninterrupted writing done, while tending to my appointment at the same time.

But just as God has done for His people all throughout the ages, on one particular afternoon during that trip, God interrupted my writing schedule to say some things to me about this particular chapter. As I entered the office for my appointment, the secretary came up the stairs to say that someone had left a message for me to call him, and it was important that I call as soon as I was free. The message was from an old family friend, a retired pastor named Dr. Rodney Allee. I had known Dr. Allee for nearly thirty years, having dated his daughter in high school and through the friendship of our families in the years that followed. So I called him from the office and agreed to meet with him at a restaurant. He said he only needed five minutes or so, but he needed to talk to me.

After I hung up, my mind went in several different directions. I knew he had recently retired, but other than that, I had no idea what he needed to meet about. I have learned through the years that no matter how busy you are or how many deadlines you are up against, there are some things, and especially some people, you clear your schedule for and allow God to interrupt your plans.

Dr. Allee and I met that afternoon, and three and a half hours later, I knew I had been in the presence of a messenger sent directly to me from the throne. The three and a half hours we spent together gave me a fire and a passion for this "authority" concept that I can hardly contain. There are a few things he said to me that day that I knew God wanted me to relate to you for your life and for such a time as this.

The first thing God said to me through this humble servant was that we are in unprecedented times and that we are on the edge of a move of God like none other. Dr. Allee had been in the ministry for over fifty years and had seen it all—the good, the bad, and the ugly. He was sent to convey to me that the church is ready, even hungry, for authentic Christianity. He told me, I believe prophetically, that the church in America is ready to move beyond experience, feelings, and just doing church and that the Lord was about to do a grassroots work whereby the church of the living God would rise up, seek Him as never before, and then assemble for war.

Now, you have to know how powerful it was to hear him say to me the very thing God had told me to write in this book. It was God not only confirming to me what He had told me to say, but it was also the Lord exhorting me to say it with more conviction, power, and force than I had originally intended. I need to stop here and tell you that Dr. Allee never knew I was writing a book at all, let alone a book on this topic, prior to this meeting.

The next thing he said really blew me away. He said, "Rich, we (the church) live in a cacophony of noise—constant sound, never stilling the soul, never calming our spirit before our God. Somehow we have got to do more of this in the church and in our daily lives." This statement completely relates to "the tipping point" that I mentioned at the end of chapter 11. In this chapter, we discussed the role of music in the church and the power of praise and worship services in the lives of the believers. What Dr. Allee said to me I have heard said by several others through the years. Author and speaker Brennen Manning has championed these silent retreats where people do not speak for three days. I have also heard about the testimonies and breakthroughs people have experienced during these times of profound silence.

Though I have never connected the dots of the messages and testimonies through the years by Manning and others, they were now connected and brought to the surface through the words Dr. Allee was saying to me.

God still speaks to His people, but if He still speaks in that still small voice, would we hear it? Could we hear it? Dr. Allee told me about a church in Denver, Colorado, that many times will conduct worship services where there is no sound at all, just silence—the reading of key Scripture passages, being still before the Lord, waiting on Him, offering up silent prayers, followed by the message from the pastor. He spoke of the profound break-throughs they were experiencing absent a "cacophony of sound." Having never thought of this when he was a pastor, he asked, "What would happen if we did that in church?"

Who knows? Is God capable of doing a new thing in the church? Would periods of silence and reflection and worship draw us closer to the throne than ever? I don't know the answers to all of these questions, but I do know one thing that God absolutely wants right now as much as ever before. He wants our steady focus and undivided attention. Time is too short, and the historical moment we find ourselves in calls for God's people to draw near, purify our hearts, and transform our thinking so that we take on His ways, carry out His thoughts, and assemble for battle.

What I do know is that the next generation is looking for something that is real, and they are not looking at our incredible church services to find it. They are looking at our lives. In the words of Ray McCauley, "If we want people to want the faith we have, they must see the quality of life it produces." After one hundred inches of rain, the bridges are out, the roads we are used to taking are no longer traversable, and there are still multitudes and multitudes in the valley of decision.

> The dogmas of the quiet past are inadequate to the stormy present.
> The occasion is piled high with difficulty, *and we must rise with the occasion.*
> And our case is new, so *we must think anew, and act anew.*[3]
> —Abraham Lincoln, emphasis added

I have to tell you one last part of my encounter with Dr. Allee. My mother works at Lockheed, and so does Dr. Allee's wife. They work a few buildings away from each other, but they see each other occasionally. I had just assumed that my mother had seen Dr. Allee's wife and that was the way he knew I was in town and knew where to find me at my appointment. When I returned home later that afternoon, I told my mother about the meeting and asked her when she had spoken to Betty (Dr. Allee's wife). She had no idea what I was talking about and had never even had a conversation or seen Betty. To this day, I cannot explain in physical terms how this meeting came to be, and I still have no idea what the "five minutes" he needed with me were for. He never said, but in the spiritual realm, I know exactly what happened and why I was to meet with Dr. Allee that day. God spoke directly to me through that humble servant of the Lord. Not as one telling me his thoughts and his ways, but as a vessel—a vessel that God spoke through to confirm and complete His work in me. Powerful stuff? You bet! But it is the stuff that is to be expected for a life lived at the next level.

chapter 15

THE HOLY SPIRIT 1:
GOD'S ULTIMATE GIFT

However, when He, the Spirit of truth, has come, He will
guide you into all truth; for He will not speak on His own
authority, but whatever He hears He will speak; and He will
tell you things to come.

—John 16:13

As I said previously, chapters 10 and 11 are the most
important writings I have ever undertaken to individual Christians,
but the most important message God has entrusted to me for the
church is the subject of the next two chapters on the Holy Spirit. These next
two chapters have been heavy on me for the last year. In some ways, I feel a bit
like Jonah on his mission to the people of Nineveh. I have spent time in the
belly of the whale. I have told God, "They will not listen," and I have asked
that someone more qualified might carry this mantle, but alas, for this next few
moments of your life, it is I that God has called to speak to you.

If I had to pick two issues that I believe have caused the greatest division in the church today, they would be the interpretation of Scripture and
the role of the Holy Spirit in the life of the believer. These two topics are
the reason we have hundreds of denominations and the reason for much of
the strife, division, and ill will that exists across denominational lines and
even within denominations. All the while, a battle is raging in the spirit
realm. The enemy is marching, and the eternal destination of millions of
souls hangs in the balance.

While it would take volumes and volumes to tackle our scriptural interpretation issues, over the next two chapters I want to unpack a lot of issues

related to the Holy Spirit and His work in the life of the believer. It is impossible to fully come under authority without acknowledging the role of the Holy Spirit in your daily walk and in your decision-making processes.

WHO IS THE HOLY SPIRIT?

Wow, that's a tough one. We know that David spoke by the power of the Holy Spirit in the Book of Psalms and that John the Baptist was filled with the Holy Spirit from birth. We know that the Book of Luke tells us that John's father, Zacharias, and his mother, Elizabeth, were both filled with the Holy Spirit at or around the time of the birth of John. All of these examples, and there are many more, were prior to the birth of Jesus and prior to the major event at Pentecost.

We also know that years later, Jesus instructed the disciples to go and wait for the Holy Spirit in the Upper Room. We know that on the Day of Pentecost the Spirit came down, touched each disciple's tongue with fire, and each person received the Holy Spirit and spoke in tongues. We also know of many other times in the New Testament when the people of God were filled with the Holy Spirit, had the Holy Spirit come upon them, or experienced similar occasions when the Holy Spirit moved in a mighty way over the lives of individual believers.

But rather than get into discussing all of the theological camps surrounding the Holy Spirit, what I would like to do is take a look at just who the Holy Spirit is in the life of the believer in the twenty-first century. Maybe we will find common ground; maybe we will not. If you think you already have all the answers to every mystery surrounding the Holy Spirit, then jump ahead two chapters or close this book and go write your own. If, however, you are truly seeking basic understanding or even deeper revelation, stick around and see what God does.

As a human being, you have two levels of consciousness, maybe more, but two that we can clearly define. One is your conscious, and the other is your subconscious. What is really interesting is that we know now that pretty much anything you have ever read, heard, learned, or experienced is stored somewhere in your subconscious, even though we can only remember or recall small amounts, but it's all there.

Suffice it to say that your conscious contains all that you can recall at a given moment, but the deepest, most painful, and most intimate parts of you are housed somewhere in your subconscious. Your soul, then, is all of you that is not physical. It is your entire spirit being, and it includes every inch of memory, experience, and every fiber of your being. In short, it is all of you. I realize that some also debate that the spirit and the soul are two different things, but for our purposes here, let's agree that the soul is the main part of us.

The Holy Spirit, on the other hand, is not confined to the whole conscious-and-subconscious thing. The Holy Spirit has it all—all of God. The Holy Spirit is the fullness of God—all of Him. The Holy Spirit is all of the deepest, most intimate, most sacred parts of our God.

Stay with me. You have to see what an incredible thing it is when the Holy Spirit comes and takes up residence inside you. When the Holy Spirit resides in you, all of a sudden, the deepest and most intimate parts of you have access and fellowship with the deepest, most intimate parts of God. Is it any wonder that Scripture says that our bodies are the *temple* of the Holy Spirit? When you ask Jesus Christ to forgive you of your sins and invite Him into your life as Lord and Savior, you have opened the door for Him to come in and live inside you. Wow!

> It is God who works in you to will and to act according to his good purpose.
>
> —Philippians 2:13, NIV

To help you understand the basic scriptural concepts related to the Holy Spirit, let's take a look at five basic principles.

Principle 1: You must acknowledge His presence.

Human reasoning will never give you God's perspective. There is so much more to the process of learning to hear God's voice. You will hear

Him if you will simply begin the process by doing one thing: acknowledge His presence. Now, I know this sounds overly simple, but think about it for a minute. When is the last time you actually spoke to the Holy Spirit that resides in you? I mean, we all acknowledge that our body is the temple of the Holy Spirit, but we go about our daily lives as if He were somewhere far off. First Corinthians 6:19–20 says, "*Or do you not know that your body is the temple of the Holy Spirit who is in you*, whom you have from God, and *you are not your own?* For you were bought at a price; therefore glorify God in your body and in your spirit, which are God's" (emphasis added).

Principle 2: Ask your questions.

Scripture says that the Holy Spirit is our teacher and our counselor. If you have a pulse, you have to have questions you would love to ask the God of the universe if given the opportunity. Well, here's your opportunity. The Holy Spirit stands waiting to not only counsel you and teach you the things of God, but He also stands ready to intercede on your behalf. "The Counselor, the Holy Spirit, whom the Father will send in my name, will teach you all things" (John 14:26, NIV). We find in Romans 8:26–27 that "the Spirit helps us in our weakness. We do not know what we ought to pray for, but the Spirit himself intercedes for us with groans that words cannot express. And he who searches our hearts knows the mind of the Spirit, because the Spirit intercedes for the saints in accordance with God's will" (NIV).

Principle 3: Allow the Spirit all access.

Whew! This is a tough one, but isn't it amazing that we think we can hide anything from God? Let's check the history on that one. First, there were Adam and Eve, then there was Achan, then, after a series of others, there was my personal favorite, Saul. That situation became so interesting when Samuel came to Saul and asked why he had not obeyed the Lord and killed everything. When Saul protested, saying that he had killed everything, Samuel replied with the phrase that never grows old: "What then is this bleating of the sheep in my ears?" (1 Sam. 15:14). He nailed him, and that was the beginning of the end for Saul.

There is nothing we can hide from God. There are things that we can internally label as "off limits" and refuse to acknowledge they are there, but that is not God's way, and He stands ready, through His Holy Spirit, to do miracles and move mountains on your behalf if you will only allow Him to do what He was sent to you to do—to liberate you and to make you all you were created to be. First Corinthians 2:10–12 says, "The Spirit searches all things, even the deep things of God. For who among men knows the thoughts of a man except the man's spirit within him? In the same way no one knows the thoughts of God except the Spirit of God. We have not received the spirit of the world but the Spirit who is from God, that we may understand what God has freely given us" (NIV).

Principle 4: Be an audience of one.

Henry Blackaby said, "The key to knowing God's voice is not a formula. It is not a method you can follow. Knowing God's voice comes from an intimate love relationship with God. That is why those who do not have the relationship do not hear what God is saying."[1] If you find yourself looking to nonbelievers or to a nonbelieving world to validate or verify your experience with God or even to confirm what is true, you will not find such validation from anyone who is not walking in the Spirit as you are in the Spirit. You must be resolved and content with an audience of One. Know this, the One (God) will never speak contrary to His Word and will always confirm what He says to you.

> *Now we have received, not the spirit of the world, but the Spirit who is from God,* that we might know the things that have been freely given to us by God. These things we also speak, not in words which man's wisdom teaches but which the Holy Spirit teaches, *comparing spiritual things with spiritual. But the natural man does not receive the things of the Spirit of God,* for they are foolishness to him; nor can he know them, *because they are spiritually discerned.* But he who is spiritual judges all things, yet he himself is rightly judged by no one. For "who has known the mind of the LORD that he may instruct Him?" *But we have the mind of Christ.*
> —1 Corinthians 2:12–16, emphasis added

Principle 5: You cannot live a lie.

The bottom line is this: you can avoid the subject of the Holy Spirit, ignore His very existence in you, and refuse to speak to Him out of some charismatic phobia you might have; nevertheless, He is there, quite possibly grieved by your capacity for independence and insensitivity, but He is not going away. Also know this: to not acknowledge His presence and to refuse to engage the One who is communing regularly with the deepest parts of you is denial at best and outright rebellion at worst, and for what? Fear of what He might cause you to do? Fear that you may experience emotions and take social risks such as openly repenting or rededicating your life to God? What is it? What could cause you to not want all God has for you? What would cause a church to simply not even discuss the six-hundred-pound gorilla in the room? Why? And, I have to speculate, at what cost to the kingdom?

> But know this, that in the last days perilous times will come: For men will be lovers of themselves, lovers of money, boasters, proud, blasphemers, disobedient to parents, unthankful, unholy, unloving, unforgiving, slanderers, without self-control, brutal, despisers of good, traitors, headstrong, haughty, lovers of pleasure rather than lovers of God, [here is the kicker] *having a form of godliness but denying its power.* And from such people turn away…*always learning and never able to come to the knowledge of the truth.*
>
> —2 Timothy 3:1–5, 7, emphasis added

You cannot get to the heart of spiritual truth absent the teaching and the counsel of the Holy Spirit, because all truth is spiritually discerned. Are you beginning to see the patterns and understand the role of the Holy Spirit in your daily life? It is the only option, and it is not just for the special "signs-and-wonders" kind of stuff. The Holy Spirit is as necessary to the Christian experience as air is to our human existence. You can ignore air all you want, but stop breathing and you will die. Refuse to breathe in the Holy Spirit, and you reduce yourself to flesh and blood, carnal man, by whatever title you choose to give yourself, including "Christian."

Carnal men and women raise up carnal churches, carnal children, and lead lives indistinguishable from those in the world. You may look different and spend your Sundays differently, but your inner spirit cries out for communion with the Spirit of God, and to deny that is to deny the God of the universe access to your very soul.

> That the righteous requirement of the law might be fulfilled in us who *do not walk according to the flesh but according to the Spirit.* For those who live according to the flesh set their minds on the things of the flesh, but those who live according to the Spirit, the things of the Spirit. *For to be carnally minded is death, but to be spiritually minded is life and peace.* Because the carnal mind is enmity against God; for it is not subject to the law of God, nor indeed can be. So then, those who are in the flesh cannot please God. *But you are not in the flesh but in the Spirit, if indeed the Spirit of God dwells in you.* Now if anyone does not have the Spirit of Christ, he is not His.
>
> —Romans 8:4–9, emphasis added

Take a moment right where you are, or get to your prayer place, and spend some time walking through these five principles again. Meditate on these principles, especially the first one. I have listed them here again for you to serve as a reminder:

Principle 1: You must acknowledge His presence.

Principle 2: Ask your questions.

Principle 3: Allow the Spirit all access.

Principle 4: Be an audience of one.

Principle 5: You cannot live a lie.

chapter 16

THE HOLY SPIRIT 2: SECONDARY SEPARATION

Therefore, indeed, I send you prophets, wise men, and scribes: some of them you will kill and crucify, and some of them you will scourge in your synagogues and persecute from city to city, that on you may come all the righteous blood shed on the earth, from the blood of righteous Abel to the blood of Zechariah, son of Berechiah, whom you murdered between the temple and the altar. Assuredly, I say to you, all these things will come upon this generation. O Jerusalem, Jerusalem, the one who kills the prophets and stones those who are sent to her! How often I wanted to gather your children together, as a hen gathers her chicks under her wings, but you were not willing! See! Your house is left to you desolate; for I say to you, you shall see Me no more till you say "Blessed is He who comes in the name of the LORD!"

—Matthew 23:34–39

HISTORY HAS SHOWN THAT THE PEOPLE WITHIN A NATION that is at war are altogether different than they are in the years of peacetime that follow the wars. In fact, in chapter 18, "Distance Theory," I explained this phenomenon in detail. Even here in the United States, we were a different people in the days immediately following the assassination of John F. Kennedy, Martin Luther King Jr., and Bobby Kennedy than we were before they were killed. In my time, we were a very different nation in the few weeks immediately following 9/11. I still have the visual picture in my mind of Democrats and Republicans gathered on the steps of the Capitol singing "God Bless America." Not too long after that, everything went back to business as usual. The Democrats hated the Republicans again, and the Republicans hated the Democrats.

The church in the United States is presently acting like a peacetime church, far removed from any threat to its freedoms and its missions. Tragically, the further we have gotten from the threat of tyranny, the more deaf and dull we have become to the intense spiritual warfare that is taking place all around us. We don't see it so much because we are so busy living the American Dream, even in the church. That is not to say that we are not busy. We are really busy. We are sending teams to all the hot spots, eager to lend a hand with cleanup and to help cities rebuild. Each of the numerous Christian nonprofits are feverishly working to save the world in each of their own hundreds of ways.

But as the church in the United States, we are a fragmented, divided lot. Our theological differences have now resulted in geographical distances and a body of Christ that is completely disconnected from its many members, each claiming to be connected to the head. There is a profound spirit of division and disunity within the collective body of Christ in the twenty-first century, and as a result, our collective voice is heard by the rest of the world only as collective noise. Problem is, the world sees the division and then gives us a D in credibility. Worse problem is, the next generation sees this same rancor and gives us an F in credibility and aspiration worthiness. We talk about peace, but all they see is division. We talk about love, and all they see is fighting.

This has not escaped the eye of our watchful Father in heaven or His Holy Spirit who lives in every believer. In the Book of Obadiah, we see a timeless message for the church in the twenty-first century. This historical event serves as a reminder of what happens when God's people turn on each other while in the midst of an attack from a foreign foe.

THE LESSON OF OBADIAH

The bitterness all began when twin brothers Esau and Jacob parted company in a dispute (Gen. 27, 32–33). Esau's descendants settled in an area called Edom while Jacob's descendants settled in Canaan and became the people of Israel. In the years that followed, there were numerous conflicts between these two factions of the same family (Num. 20:14–21). During a twenty-year period (605–586 B.C.) the Babylonians invaded the southern kingdom of Judah and of Israel, making several attacks on the sacred city of Jerusalem, which was finally devastated in 586 B.C. The Edomites (Esau's descendants), rather than putting aside years of division and territorial squabbles and standing with their brother's household, instead saw an opportunity to get even with their distant relatives and joined with the Babylonians in the slaughter. In the process, they helped desecrate the land of Judah. Three different books of the Bible decry the role the Edomites played in the destruction of Jerusalem (Ps. 137:7; Lam. 4:21–22; Ezek. 25:12–14). Enter Obadiah, God's prophet to the Edomites:

> For violence against your brother Jacob,
> Shame shall cover you,
> And you shall be cut off forever.
> In the day that you stood on the other side—
> In the day that strangers carried captive his forces,
> When foreigners entered his gates
> And cast lots for Jerusalem—
> Even you were as one of them.
> But you should not have gazed on the day of your brother
> In the day of his captivity;
> Nor should you have rejoiced over the children of Judah
> In the day of their destruction;
> Nor should you have spoken proudly
> In the day of distress...
> For the day of the LORD upon all the nations is near;
> As you have done, it shall be done to you;
> Your reprisal shall return upon your own head.
> —Obadiah 10–12, 15, emphasis added

SECONDARY SEPARATION

The separation issue comes from the scriptural examples where inter-marrying with foreign women led to paganism and idol worship. The New Testament mandate comes from Ephesians 5:8–11: "For you were once darkness, but now you are light in the Lord. Walk as children of light... finding out what is acceptable to the Lord. And have no fellowship with the unfruitful works of darkness, but rather expose them."

Secondary separation is a position taken whereby a denomination or a church deems it necessary, due to doctrinal disagreement, to separate from another denomination or church. This separation includes involvement even on issues or situations where both are in agreement. For example, a church decides that it cannot have fellowship with another church because that church believes in speaking in tongues, believing that the tongues group is spreading false-teaching or even heresy. Titles like "heretic," "false teachers," and "apostates" are given out with ease and with the conviction of an inquisition, a witch trial, or a town hanging. Problem is, when we do that, we are no better than the Moabites. Worse problem is, God's track record for these kinds of things is pretty clear.

So where do we go from here? I know where I go from here. I have been sent by the Lord to give a strong warning to the church in the United States, the millions of individual followers of Christ, and the message to the millions of Christ followers is simply this: we are at war. The enemy is all around us and is taking more and more ground every day—children, families, marriages, unborn children, and the multitudes in the valley of decision. This is not the time for arguments over hermeneutics, contextual interpretation, and heated discussions over the five pillars of Calvinism. United, we are a mighty army. Divided, we are just a self-serving, highly spirited debate club living in our own individual, theological, man-made camps.

The topic of the Holy Spirit comes center stage when the discussion of bringing down the walls comes up. On both sides of the wall reside powerful men and women of God who have been used by God mightily. Let's take a look at what we are allowing to divide us when it comes to the subject of the Holy Spirit. Basically, there are three pivotal issues that have divided the church:

1. A second baptism or filling experience
2. Speaking in tongues
3. Healing

And really, when it comes down to it, all parties agree that God can heal whomever He wants to heal, any way he wants to do it. The division comes when a person assumes this role. Then the sparks fly, but let's eliminate this topic as there is at least some common ground. That leaves us with the big two: second baptism and tongues. Here is where a shift in focus needs to take place. Both sides of this issue firmly hold to their long-held positions, which is fine, but what we miss in the battle of words is the move of God in and through men and women on both sides of this man-made fence. Take a look at some of the players and where they fall in relation to these two specific topics:

No Second Baptism and Tongues	Baptism and Tongues Scriptural
Billy Graham	Mark Rutland
Jack Hyles	Jack Hayford
D. L. Moody	Chuck Smith
Jerry Falwell	Hillsong
Charles Stanley	T. D. Jakes
Adrian Rogers	Ray McCauley
John MacArthur	Joyce Meyer

I could literally write volumes on each one listed, both columns filled with miracles, crusades, and the millions of souls who have been won through these mighty warriors for the Lord. They are all known by their fruit and have a legacy of soul-winning and life change that is indisputable.

So why do we miss that in all of our debate and nasty discourse? I know why. For the same reasons the Pharisees did. Time after time, Jesus would do a miracle, not just any miracle but incredible miracles. Each time there would be a Pharisee or two standing by who would witness the miracle and have no recognition, appreciation, or sense of awe at the miracle they had just witnessed with their own eyes. Instead, they went running back to tell the council of some technicality in the Law that Jesus had broken. They were present for a miracle but only saw a violation. They were in the presence of the living God but chose to measure Him by their narrow understanding of who God was and what He could do.

Here we are in the twenty-first century doing the same thing. To say that Billy Graham is not "filled" with the Spirit and therefore is missing it big-time is to miss the very power of God when it is right in your face. Conversely, to hear just one testimony from any of Dr. Mark Rutland's missionary journeys and feel he is a false teacher or a heretic because of his belief in speaking in tongues being for today is to also miss the point entirely. In the process, we become like the very people who crucified Christ.

> Let them do good, that they be rich in good works, ready to give, willing to share, storing up for themselves a good foundation for the time to come, that they may lay hold on eternal life. O Timothy! Guard what was committed to your trust, avoiding the profane and idle babble and contradictions of what is falsely called knowledge—by possessing it some have strayed concerning the faith. Grace be with you. Amen.
> —1 Timothy 6:18–21

I could walk through each and every name written above and tell you miracle after miracle, souls upon souls who have been rescued through their ministries. Some are so incredibly conservative it would shock you, and others speak in tongues every time they minister. Both groups are doing immeasurably well in the kingdom, with fruit to show for their efforts and lives that have stood the test of time. After all, in a few years, in just a vapor of time, we will all see clearly anyway, won't we? In heaven there will be no division, and truth will be obvious to all. So why not pray today, "Thy kingdom come, Thy will be done, TODAY, on Earth as it is in heaven?"

If the only common ground we shared was the following few tenets of the faith, we could change the world—together.

- Jesus was born of a virgin.
- Jesus's died, was buried, and resurrected from the dead.
- Jesus was the Son of God made flesh.
- There is a heaven and a hell.
- All who do not acknowledge Jesus as the Son of God and invite Him to be their Lord and Savior are condemned to an eternity in hell.
- The only path to salvation is through Jesus Christ.
- Scripture is God's Word for every generation, accurate in all its content, written by God through the hands of men
- All who come to Christ as Savior need to publicly testify to that through water baptism.
- Jesus will return.

Wow! That is a lot to unite under, and millions of souls hang in the balance in need of a Savior. The Book of Matthew says this of Jesus when He looked out over the multitudes: "Then Jesus went about all the cities and villages, teaching in their synagogues, preaching the gospel of the kingdom, and healing every sickness and every disease among the people. *But when He saw the multitudes, He was moved with compassion for them,* because they were weary and scattered, like sheep having no shepherd. Then He said to His disciples, '*The harvest truly is plentiful, but the laborers are few. Therefore pray the Lord of the harvest to send out laborers into His harvest*'" (Matt. 9:35–38, emphasis added).

This is not a season for lone rangers—individuals or churches. Nor is it a time for debate and endless dialogue over issues completely unrelated to the harvest in need of laborers. We must teach our people about the power and the role of the Holy Spirit in the lives of the believer unashamedly and in good measure, for He is the very teacher, counselor, and intercessor they need for such a time as this. Let's leave the intricacies and the differences in doctrine at the door. May these lesser issues not divide us, and may Satan awake to find a unified move of God as he has never seen before—all under the authority of our living God, empowered by His precious and mighty Holy Spirit.

Finally, all of you be of one mind, having compassion for one another; love as brothers, be tenderhearted, be courteous; not returning evil for evil or reviling for reviling, but on the contrary blessing, knowing that you were called to this, that you may inherit a blessing. For "He who would love life and see good days, let him refrain his tongue from evil, and his lips from speaking deceit. Let him turn away from evil and do good; *let him seek peace and pursue it. For the eyes of the* LORD *are on the righteous, and His ears are open to their prayers*; but the face of the LORD is against those who do evil."

—1 Peter 3:8–12, emphasis added

SECTION 5

THE GREAT AWAKENING— A CALL TO ARMS

And do this, knowing the time, that now it is high time to awake out of sleep; for now our salvation is nearer than when we first believed. The night is far spent, the day is at hand. Therefore let us cast off the works of darkness, and let us put on the armor of light. Let us walk properly, as in the day, not in revelry and drunkenness, not in lewdness and lust, not in strife and envy. But put on the Lord Jesus Christ, and make *no* provision for the flesh, to fulfill its lusts.

—Romans 13:11–14, emphasis added

chapter 17

LESSONS LEARNED

Therefore keep watch, because you do not know on what day
your Lord will come. But understand this: If the owner of the
house had known at what time of night the thief was coming,
he would have kept watch and would not have let his house
be broken into. So you must also be ready, because the Son of
Man will come at an hour when you do not expect him.

—Matthew 24:42–44, NIV

O K; WE HAVE SOME GOOD NEWS AND SOME BAD NEWS. THE
bad news is that the army of Satan is marching. The threat is
real, his objective is clear, and his methods are almost invisible
to the naked eye. Good news is, God is on the move. Nothing escapes His
ever-watchful eyes, and He is moving in ways that are absolutely visible to
the naked eye—if one will simply look.

I believe that one of the most important steps to victory for any critical
situation is the simple acknowledgment that there is a problem. Until this is
realized and acknowledged, there is no reason to meet, no reason to develop
a strategy to solve the problem, and no reason to even become concerned.
As much as we all love to be proactive and foresee potential threats and
downturns, they inevitably happen. They happen in every business, in every
institution, and in every family.

But what we are dealing with here is not something that can be stopped
by simply being proactive. That ship has sailed. What I am talking about
is an imminent threat; the enemy, Satan and his demonic forces, living
and moving freely among us. How did we get here? Simply put, we face an
incredibly patient adversary in a very impatient and results-oriented society.
We have been asleep spiritually. The church has slept through some of the

most critical decisions and movements of Satan in the history of the world. We have been the frog in the hot water. The pot gradually gets hotter and hotter, until at last, when it is too late, he succumbs to a death he did not see coming, never thinking to do what he does best—leap.

NEXT-LEVEL TRUTH

Now, I think it is only fair to pause here for a moment and reexamine one of the most powerful next-level truths that exist. True next-level living requires a basic understanding that there are two worlds: (1) a physical world where we can see, touch, taste, smell, and hear, and (2) and a spirit world—invisible to the naked eye but absolutely as real as the physical world. It is in this realm that so much is going on. It is here that a war is raging for the souls of man. The strategy, as stated before, is to win the mind of man and the children of man. Our little ones are at stake.

Now, I am not talking spooky, haunted-house kind of stuff. I am talking about the kind of stuff that's real and in the Bible. Jesus talked about it and addressed it. In fact, it is because of the activity that exists in this world that we should be living a life at the next level. It is not simply a luxury; it is required of anyone who seeks to go deeper and to stand in the gap for their family and an unbelieving nation.

HISTORICAL RELEVANCE

When it comes to examining the people of God over the centuries, history holds incredible lessons for us in the forms of patterns of behavior that repeat themselves again and again. The people of God, from Adam and Eve until now, are no exceptions. In fact, we are the rule. The progression of God's people throughout history is filled with time periods or eras and the prevailing voices of those eras or time periods. If we would only look for the patterns that emerge, we would discover some amazing parallels to where we are today. Again, same problems, different day, infinitely multiplied.

Any student of biblical history will tell you that the people of God, from the very beginning, have struggled with three critical issues:

1. Lust of the eye
2. A constant pull to false gods
3. The desire for flesh-and-blood leaders, who by the simple fact that they are human are then subject to the blessings of the righteous and the discipline of the unrighteous. I refer to these men and women as "the generals," and in Scripture they were often kings and priests.

The lust of the eye

Nothing has withheld God's hand of blessing more than simple flesh-and-blood, lust-of-the-eye kind of stuff. Whether it was Adam and Eve in the garden, Achan in the tent, Samson with Delilah, David on the balcony, or the church at Corinth, the lust of the eye has felled the greatest kings, murdered the mightiest warriors, and brought down many a pastor from the pulpit. Same problem, different day, infinitely multiplied.

False gods

One of the most frustrating patterns in the Old Testament is God's people and their besetting sin of pursuing and worshiping false gods. We watch and see the very people who saw God part the Red Sea, receive manna from heaven, and do signs and wonders all around them, and they still bowed down to a cow made of gold. Generation after generation, the people of God found themselves being carried away, either through their attraction to foreign women or simply by the evil desires of their own hearts. They forsook the God of their youth, the God of their heritage, and bowed down to images made by the hands of man.

In today's terms, this is called idolatry, and we actually are no better today than our predecessors when it comes to aligning our passions, our time, and our finances to the things of the earth, while leaving little for the God of the universe. A simple drive around town on a Sunday morning will reveal all you need to see to know that man has chosen for himself a religion that is not housed in a church and gods made by human hands.

The desire for flesh-and-blood leaders

> Then all the elders of Israel gathered together and came to Samuel at Ramah, and said to him, "Look, you are old, and your sons do not walk in your ways. Now make us a king to judge us like all the nations." But the thing displeased Samuel when they said, "Give us a king to judge us." So Samuel prayed to the LORD. And the LORD said to Samuel, "Heed the voice of the people in all that they say to you; for they have not rejected you, but they have rejected Me, that I should not reign over them. According to all the works which they have done since the day that I brought them out of Egypt, even to this day—with which they have forsaken Me and served other gods—so they are doing to you also. Now therefore, heed their voice. However, you shall solemnly forewarn them, and show them the behavior of the king who will reign over them."
>
> —1 Samuel 8:4–9

Then, after Samuel warned the people in as stern and as harsh of terms he could muster, the reply of the people was not only astounding, but it sets the stage for all that has happened since and all that is happening even today in the twenty-first century. Verse 19 picks up with this: "Nevertheless the people refused to obey the voice of Samuel; and they said, 'No, but we will have a king over us, that we also may be like all the nations, and that our king may judge us and go out before us and fight our battles.' And Samuel heard all the words of the people, and he repeated them in the hearing of the LORD. So the LORD said to Samuel, 'Heed their voice, and make them a king.' And Samuel said to the men of Israel, 'Every man go to his city'" (1 Sam. 8:19–22).

It is critical that you remember those words: "…and that our king may judge us and go out before us and fight our battles."

THE MODERN-DAY GENERALS IN EVANGELICAL CHRISTIANITY

This is the era that we find ourselves in the twenty-first century. We, the evangelical church in the United States, are a people being led largely by generals. A few are self-appointed quacks, but most are godly, awesome warriors for Christ. Thousands are local pastors and church leaders and incredible parachurch organizations such as Focus on the Family, Christian Coalition, or National Association of Evangelicals. Many of these are led and staffed by godly, wise men and women serving Christ all across the nation. Meanwhile, the rank-and-file Christian goes about life as usual in pursuit of the American Dream, with the hope and desire for a king or for a general in our case today, that he or she might "go out before us and fight our battles" in the kingdom.

Problem is, just as in the days of Samuel, this was never God's plan. Answer is, His plan for the church in the twenty-first century is never to leave the fighting to the generals and their staff, but rather for the rank-and-file Christian to become spiritually attuned and obedient to the voice of God as He is heard through the many modes and channels available, that they may grow right where they are planted, alongside the army of God—all hearing one voice, following one path, and attuned to the things of the Spirit.

In the next chapter, I will show you how this has played out over the course of the last half of the twentieth century. Then I will show you how this repeated cycle has led us to where we are today. For now, suffice it to say that while we slumbered and while we were at the play, the enemy took ground and entrenched himself in high places—places once reserved for the people of God. In his wake, death of an ideal, a way of life even, was lost to the enemy. Think I'm exaggerating? Look and see for yourself the damage done as two major wars and 185 years of faithful service and leadership by God's people in all of the most influential sectors of life were not enough to stem the tide of an approaching army besieging a sleeping foe.

chapter 18

DISTANCE THEORY

And he will turn many of the children of Israel to the Lord their God. He will also go before Him in the spirit and the power of Elijah, "to turn the hearts of the fathers to the children," and the disobedient to the wisdom of the just, to make ready a people prepared for the Lord.

—Luke 1:16–17

CHRISTIAN AUTHOR, RESEARCHER, AND PUBLISHER CHUCK Missler publishes a monthly update from his ministry called Koinonia House, based in Post Falls, Idaho. His monthly newsletter is filled with fascinating facts and research on topics that range from the political arena to Bible prophecy and historical exposition. It was his October 2000 edition that caught my eye when I first stumbled across it. In an article entitled, "Twilight's Last Gleaming?" Chuck had done a considerable amount of research on the history of great civilizations of ages past and present. What he discovered is both fascinating and frightening. He states: "There is a view among some historians that a democracy is an intrinsically unstable form of government." The article goes on to report that "a democracy cannot exist as a permanent form of government."[1]

And here is the frightening part: *the average age of the world's greatest civilizations is two hundred years.* Well, simple math puts us at somewhere near two hundred forty years old. To a certain extent, we are in uncharted waters. What the article goes on to uncover is that those waters aren't as uncharted as we might think. In fact, all great civilizations have followed the same progression, each with the same tragic results. Chuck explains it like this:

The cycle [of a civilization or a nation] is surprisingly predict-able…"from bondage to spiritual faith; from spiritual faith to great courage; from courage to liberty; from liberty to abundance; from abundance to complacency; from complacency to apathy; from apathy to dependency; from dependency back again into bondage."[2]

I have given you a diagram of this cycle as a visual aid to help see this progression. Where are we? Many religious leaders in this country would place us somewhere between apathy and dependency.[3]

WHERE ARE WE?

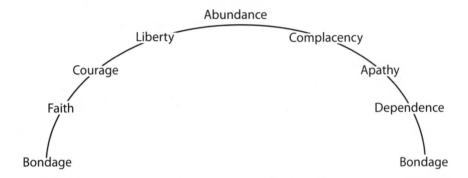

Can you see why so many of our nation's religious leaders, biblical scholars, and pastors are so concerned? Can you see why they are increasingly devoting so much of their time and prayer life to asking God to keep His hand of judgment on this nation? They can see it. George Barna, Christian researcher and student of American trends, states: "America is rapidly devolving into a society beset by moral anarchy." In his volume *Boiling Point*, he flatly states that moral anarchy has arrived and rules our culture today. "The argument hinges on a substantial amount of attitudinal and behavioral evidence: record bankruptcy levels, frivolous lawsuits, the rapid growth of the pornography industry, highway speeding as the norm, income tax cheating, computer hacking and viruses, rising levels of white collar crime, rampant copyright violations (movies, books, recordings), terrorism and intimidation tactics, net-based plagiarism, emotional comfort with lying and cheating, increasing rates of co-habitation and adultery, and so forth."4

THE CHURCH: GOD'S INSTRUMENT OF HOPE FOR THE WORLD

The evidence is overwhelming. Were it not for Christians in this country and around the world on their knees daily seeking God's mercy, there would be little that would stand between sinful man and a righteous and just God. I want to also proclaim that I have personally stood in congregations across this country where they are winning this war. Their youth programs are alive and vibrant. Their worship is filled with excitement, enthusiasm, and joy. Scripture is being proclaimed with boldness and power, and the lost are being found and redeemed. God is alive and moving in their midst, and they are experiencing victory. There is hope, there is joy, and there is redemptive community! I have seen it.

THE EUROPEAN EXPERIMENT—THE ROAD TO NOWHERE

Throughout history, Europe was home to some of the greatest moves of God ever to happen on Planet Earth. Some of the greatest revivals in history were held in Europe as thousands upon thousands jammed the cathedrals and stormed the aisles for salvation. Some revivals went on for weeks, watching the Lord move with great might and power.

But it never took root in the halls of government, the courts of the land, or the universities of the day. In fact, the move of the Holy Spirit was so strong during that time, that many great denominational leaders, out of jealousy and pride, began to pick apart these mighty moves of God, dismissing them as fake, false, and ill-conceived. At a time when denominations should have locked arms and taken a nation by storm, they instead argued over the validity of the decisions and the methods of the evangelists.

Fast-forward to the twenty-first century, and you now have in Europe one of the most liberal, godless countries on the face of the planet. Secularism has become the model, with its offers of freedom and tolerance for all. Great cathedrals filled with worshipers have now been turned into shopping centers, restaurants, and hotels filled with shoppers and tourists. The very blood of the martyrs still resides in the cracks of those famed floors, only to be trampled on by a people who know not their God.

The result is a nation more at risk militarily, socially, and morally than at any other time in its history. It is a nation besieged by violence and widely divided along social, racial, socioeconomical, and cultural boundaries. The "grand experiment" has failed, and with it, hundreds of years of history. Millions of souls later, it stands for everything that can happen to a nation of Christians who choose to slumber on or live only within the hallowed halls of the marketplace.

Thousands of miles away in the United States, the Christian church has slept through much of the past fifty years while the enemy crept in among us, moved into strategic positions of power and influence, and, little by little, changed the very fabric of our society—one law, one ruling, one new idea at a time.

We slept while the enemy marched on some of our most treasured ground. That ground is now a fortress, held by an enemy that never sleeps. His recipe for success is to simply sit by and let man be man. He knows that sooner or later man's selfish pride and his longing to live the American Dream will cause him to abandon the hallowed halls that made those dreams come true in order to pursue affluence and leisure.

chapter 19

SURRENDERED GROUND

Make no mistake. The sixties were not just an era of long hair and bell-bottoms. It was an intellectual and cultural upheaval that marked the end of modernity's optimism and introduced the worldview of despair on a broad level. Ideas concocted in the rarefied domain of academia filtered down to shape an entire generation of young people. They, in turn, have brought those ideas to their logical conclusion in postmodernism, *with its suspicion of the very notions of reason and objective truth.*[1]

—Chuck Colson, emphasis added

W AY BACK IN 1776, SOME OF THE BRAVEST AND MOST VISIONARY men to ever walk the face of the earth established a nation with documents and covenants that would not only stand the test of time but would also weather some of the most incredible storms ever to assail a movement. This was truly rarefied air, "lightning-in-a-bottle" kind of stuff, resulting in the Declaration of Independence, the Constitution, the Bill of Rights, and a system of government that still stands as the model for free nations of the world. Every inch of ground gained during these sacred moments of history was gained not only by the blood of men and women in the fray but also by the sustaining hand of God.

For the next 180 years or so, Christian men and women inhabited the highest offices in the land, ran the most prestigious universities, and served their country as elected politicians and representatives of the people. Throughout over two hundred thirty years of existence, there have been six major entities that have sustained and maintained the American way of life. They are the universities, the legislative branch, the judicial branch, the executive branch, public schools, and the marketplace.

During this time period of establishment and maintaining our freedoms (roughly 1776–1955), each of these six areas of public life in the United States was filled with Christian men and women with Christian ideals, Christian values, and Christ-honoring objectives, but as early as 1960, something very interesting began to take place. Suddenly, an entirely different set of faces began to emerge, and the struggle for values and ideas began.

THE GREAT ESCAPE

It was during the next fifteen to twenty years (1960–1980) that something else of great importance began to emerge. As the population grew and as church denominations grew to megapower status, the people of God repeated a cycle not seen since the time of Saul and David. The people of God began to abandon the public square, beating a quick path to the marketplace in pursuit of—you guessed it—the American Dream.

The thought was the same as it was many years ago: our generals are strong, they are fully armed, and they speak for me. "Let our generals do our fighting for us." And in our (Christianity's) rush to the marketplace, we left in our wake a huge leadership vacuum, one soon to be filled by men and women who did not—*do not*—share our ideals, our Christian values, or our standards. Worse yet, they do not follow the God of Israel or bow a knee to His Son, Jesus.

In that brief twenty-year period, the Christians in this nation, without even so much as a good fight, exchanged influence for affluence, and leadership for leisure. In the next twenty years (1980–2000), this was infinitely multiplied.

Influence --------- exchanged for ⟶ *Affluence*

Leadership -------- exchanged for ⟶ *Leisure*

This disastrous exchange of societal values for personal gain has had far-reaching effects on society, especially as it relates to the American family. How so? Simple. Did you know, for example, that the percentage of Americans working in professions and jobs that bore them to tears and leave them unfulfilled is staggeringly high?[2] So why do it? Affluence and leisure—and debt—make it almost impossible to even consider any career change that does not equal or exceed current financial status.

How does this affect the family? Well, that's an easy one to prove. When people do not find fulfillment in their careers and in the workplace, they find it elsewhere, and that usually means things, more things. Problem is, that doesn't satisfy either, at least, not for long. This results in frustrated, overextended men and women seeking fulfillment, meaning, and adventure in all the wrong places. Did you know that financial stress is one of the leading causes for divorce in the United States? Does financial and marital stress affect our children? Absolutely!

Question is, how many gifted teachers are selling insurance? I wonder how many gifted minds settle way too early in life for a quick buck, exchanging knowledge for cash and purpose for a quick fix or thrill.

One of those brave souls who dared exchange financial gain for purpose and a call was my friend Jeff. Jeff was a very successful businessman all through the 1980s and 1990s. By all standards he was a very successful man with a big house, a loving family, and even a Mercedes Benz. There was only one problem: Jeff knew way down in his knower that while he could be successful in this field, in his inner man and in his spirit he was miserable, but he was not miserable because he hated his job. He was miserable simply because he knew what he had a passion to do, and he wasn't doing it.

Now, this created a dilemma on several different levels. He did not have a teaching certificate or any real college training that would entitle him to be considered for 99 percent of all teaching jobs. So, with great faith, Jeff put out the résumés and began the search for meaning, for something to do with the one life he'd been given to live. Finally, after much searching, he found a school that would give him a chance. His big break had arrived at a whopping twenty-five thousand dollars per year, thousands below his current standard of living.

Over the next five years, Jeff not only became the most popular teacher in the school, but he also became one of the most successful salesmen ever. He sold his house, his television, his car, his furniture, and so on. Now, of course I am joking, but suffice it to say, he and his family sacrificed a great deal as he would teach until 3:30 p.m. and then give violin lessons until 6:00 p.m. Wealthy? Nope, not anymore. Happy? Fulfilled? Valued? You bet! Now, just six years later, he not only teaches every week, but he is also the children's pastor at a church near his home. The finances have come with each new year living his dream.

Jeff has a very natural gift of teaching and working with children. One would have to wonder how many adults never truly do what they were created to do because it does not fit the financial goals they have set for themselves. We work backwards. Instead of looking for the jobs that fit our financial goals, we should be looking for vocations that fit our call and then adjust our lives to the financial picture that it paints. The key? What brings greater satisfaction—what one does from nine to five each week or the things one can own and use occasionally?

Thus our dilemma: a race to the marketplace only to find it is not at all the stuff of life and purpose and adventure. In the end, we leave the more noble causes like our education institutions, our courts, and our government to men and women who have discovered there is greater worth found in shaping the course of a nation or a community than there is stringing together the best set of cars, houses, and toys.

The implications on a social and psychological level are very telling as well. One example is the grip depression has on so many American adults— Americans living in the wealthiest nation on the planet. According to a 2007 *Newsweek* article called "Men and Depression, Facing the Darkness," at least six million men will be diagnosed with depression this year alone.[3] This is in addition to the millions more that will continue to suffer silently. The article continues:

> The result is a hidden epidemic of despair that is destroying marriages, disrupting careers, filling jail cells, clogging emergency rooms, and

costing society billions of dollars in lost productivity and medical bills. The annual economic impact of adult depression is estimated at $83 billion in lost productivity.

If only they knew that our God stands ready to meet them right where they are with hope, a plan, and a purpose. Psalm 34:18 says, "The LORD *is* close to the brokenhearted; he rescues those who are crushed in spirit" (NLT, emphasis added).

This leads us to the twenty-first century, with our schools that defy the very existence of our God, refusing to even acknowledge His presence or His role in our science books, or His hand in the formation of this once-great country. They have filled our judicial benches with far too many judges who have no regard for the sanctity of human life or its Creator and have filled our government halls with sandpaper and chisels, ridding our national state houses of any and all reference to the Ten Commandments or to the God who gave the victory at the outset.

Meanwhile, we eat, drink, and make merry much like the frog in the boiling water. We see the violence and the radical elements marching around the globe as the death tolls rise almost daily, but that is in someone else's land. We live as though we are completely blind to the signs of the times and the movement of our God as He calls His people out of their slumber and into the fray as, once again, we leave the fighting to the generals.

We must wake the church. We must sound the alarm, and we must heed the call to get ready. The British are coming! The enemy is marching, and we must slumber no more.

> Superficiality is the curse of our age. The doctrine of instant satisfaction is primarily a spiritual problem. The desperate need today is not for a greater number of intelligent people, or gifted people, but for deep people.[4]
>
> —Richard Foster

In other words, the need in the kingdom is for men and women who can see beyond their circumstances and beyond the superficiality of affluence and leisure and begin to see the enemy in our midst. We must begin to see all that God is doing in the spirit realm, in a place I call the next level.

chapter 20

OUR FIXED POINT OF REFERENCE: SOMEWHERE BETWEEN TIME AND ETERNITY

In many parts of contemporary culture, it is acceptable to believe in God, but only if you keep your belief in a private box. Yet Christianity will not remain privatized. It is not merely a personal belief. It is the truth about all reality. Christians must learn how to break out of the box, to penetrate environments hostile to our faith, make people see the dilemma they themselves face, and then show them why the Christian worldview is the only rational answer.[1]

—Chuck Colson

NOW, I HAVE TO PAUSE HERE AND MAKE SOMETHING VERY CLEAR. This is *not* a book about social change. This is not written with the goal of revolutionary societal change and a shift in public thinking. On the contrary, this is about something much bigger—our fixed position in time, God's time, and the timetable of scriptural history. The situation we find ourselves in is no surprise to God, nor should it be to you. We are very much a society that mirrors the society before the flood and the society in Sodom and Gomorrah just prior to the fire and brimstone. We live in a world that is described in great detail through the Old and New Testament prophets when they talk about the second coming of Jesus Christ.

But this is also not just a book about the End Times. I really do not know with certainty that Jesus is coming back tomorrow, or the next day, or the next day. I just believe, based on the evidence, that He's coming back soon, and I'm not alone in this conclusion. Also, I do know this: we are certainly a society on the brink of God's judgment, socially and spiritually. We are a people who, having a basic understanding of the prophetic, know that most of the prophecy that is to take place prior to Christ's return has happened. So somewhere between the judgment prophesied in Ezekiel and Joel and the Second Coming prophesied in Daniel and Revelation sleeps a slumbering giant called the church, the bride of Christ, a chosen people, and a royal priesthood—us.

THE URGENCY OF THE HOUR

Now—and this *is* what the book is about—what Scripture and history teach us is that there is a time period prior to the Second Coming in a society that very much resembles our own. It is in that time period that I believe we find ourselves. Problem is, we do not know how long it will last. Good news is, none of the evil stuff of the earth can stop what God has planned during this late hour—an outpouring of the Holy Spirit, incredible moves of God through His people, and a harvest of epic proportions.

> In the last days, God says, I will pour out my Spirit on all people. Your sons and daughters will prophesy, your young men will see visions, your old men will dream dreams. Even on my servants, both men and women, I will pour out my Spirit in those days, and they will prophesy. I will show wonders in the heaven above and signs on the earth below, blood and fire and billows of smoke. The sun will be turned to darkness and the moon to blood before the coming of the great and glorious day of the Lord. And everyone who calls on the name of the Lord will be saved.
>
> —Acts 2:17–21, NIV

> The rise of terrorism in our world and the emerging crisis in the Middle East between Israel and Iran are part of a much bigger picture—that of God's plan for the future of Israel and the entire world.[2]
>
> —End-Times Expert John Hagee

That is why it is so critical that we grasp the urgency of the hour we are in as well as the obstacles that lie before us. The army of Satan is marching, but our God is moving, and He is calling each of us to great acts of courage, obedience, and action. According to the words of the prophet Joel, there are "multitudes, multitudes in the valley of decision" (Joel 3:14). A harvest is there for the picking, but who will do the picking?

> But when He [Jesus] saw the multitudes, He was moved with compassion for them, because they were weary and scattered, like sheep having no shepherd. Then He said to His disciples, "The harvest truly is plentiful, but the laborers are few. Therefore pray the Lord of the harvest to send out laborers into His harvest."
>
> —Matthew 9:36–38

> Jesus said to them, "My food is to do the will of Him who sent Me, and to finish His work. Do you not say, 'There are four months and then comes the harvest'? Behold I say to you, lift up your eyes and look at the fields, for they are already white for harvest! And he who reaps receives wages, and gathers fruit for eternal life, that both he who sows and he who reaps may rejoice together. For in this the saying is true: 'One sows and another reaps.' I sent you to reap that for which you have not labored; others have labored, and you have entered into their labors."
>
> —John 4:34–38

> Then I looked, and behold, a white cloud, and on the cloud sat One like the Son of Man, having on His head a golden crown, and in His hand a sharp sickle. And another angel came out of the temple, crying with a loud voice to Him who sat on the cloud, "Thrust in Your sickle and reap, for the time has come for You to reap, for the harvest of the earth is ripe." So He who sat on the cloud thrust in His sickle on the earth, and the earth was reaped.
>
> —Revelation 14:14–16

As I write this book, we as a nation are on the brink of a political revolution that could result in a social revolution. We stand at the same door

Europe stood at not too many years ago. We are knocking on the door of a godless government and purely secular discourse. There's no room for Jesus at this inn, either. While I certainly am not endorsing one political party over another, just a quick examination of the agenda of those who stand ready to ascend Capitol Hill reveals sweeping change and a severe shift to the left of center—politically, socially, and morally.

Why is it important to shift our eyes to the coming secular agenda? Because as it becomes legal, it then becomes educational. As it becomes educational, it beckons a call for greater understanding and acceptance. As the cry for greater understanding and acceptance intensifies, the message ultimately finds its way into the classrooms in the United States, and the indoctrination begins. In fact, in many states, it is already embedded in the curriculum, embraced by the school administrations, and woven into the fabric of society. This secular agenda includes the homosexual agenda, safe sex, and its cousins, abortion and sexually transmitted diseases.

The most powerful nation on the planet possesses the highest suicide rate, the highest prison populations, and the highest levels of chemical dependency of any nation on the earth. According to the U.S. Bureau of Justice Statistics and the U.S. Census Bureau, one in thirty-two adults in the United States is under corrections supervision. In Georgia, one in every fifteen adults is under corrections supervision. (Correction supervision refers to those in prison or on some kind of probation and/or monitoring).[3]

Democracy or any other form of government absent God of the universe, simply does not work. When will the church wake up and see the coming threat, hear the thundering sound of an approaching army, and rally to the cause of Christ for the next generation and for the "multitudes, multitudes in the valley of decision"?

Make no mistake; we are in those days. You can call them the last days or whatever you want to call them, but we are there, and the war is on! Never forget what's at stake or the enemy's objective. It is the same objective as ours: to win the mind of man and the children of man, our little ones—the next generation. That is the battleground, and that is the prize. Whoever controls the mind and the moral compass of the next generation changes the tide of public opinion and determines the true north for everything religious, spiritual, and what is "normal and acceptable behavior" for the era to come.

DIG IN

Perhaps you have had a moment of revelation and have experienced an awakening after reading all of this. Perhaps you were there before you read one word. The questions I have been sent by God to ask are these: Are you in? Are you willing to get all the way in? Do you see what is coming, and are you committed enough to the cause of Christ to go for it? Are you ready to go to the next level? If the answer is yes to any or all of these questions, then take a moment right where you are and tell Him. Tell Him in the simplest of terms, "I'm in!"

If you prayed that prayer and are ready to get all the way in and fight for your little ones and for the kingdom and if you are ready for whatever God is about to do, then the rest of this book is devoted to walking you through the next steps to prepare you for battle. Dig in. Commit the next twenty to thirty days or so to this cause, and prepare for war. The path is set. A journey is about to begin, and when you come out on the other side, one thing is for certain: you will not be the same person you were when you began.

chapter 21

One Hundred Inches of Rain: The Aftermath of a Storm

> History will have to record that the greatest tragedy of this period of social transition was not the strident clamor of the bad people, but the appalling silence of the good people.[1]
>
> —Martin Luther King Jr.

> Human progress is neither automatic nor inevitable. Every step toward the goal of justice requires sacrifice, suffering, and struggle; the tireless exertions and passionate concern of dedicated individuals.[2]
>
> —Martin Luther King Jr.

I N THE FALL OF 1998, AN INCREDIBLE STORM SWEPT ACROSS THE ocean, heading directly for the coast of Honduras. The storm quickly evolved to hurricane status. By the time it reached land, it was of such size and magnitude that terror gripped that tiny nation as thousands hunkered down and hoped for the best. By the time Hurricane Mitch finished with Honduras, the damage was enormous, the implications for life after the storm were almost unimaginable, and life as they once knew it was gone forever. The aftermath of Hurricane Mitch read like a horror novel:[3]

- Over nine thousand died.
- Over nine thousand were missing.
- Ninety-two bridges were destroyed.
- Fifty percent of the country's agricultural production was destroyed.
- Over seventy thousand houses were destroyed.
- Over 1.9 million were injured.

- More than one million were left homeless.
- Major cities were isolated.
- Over five thousand lived on rooftops for several days.
- Fifty years of progress destroyed.

When a nation goes through a storm of this magnitude, there are certain things that happen in the aftermath of that storm that are extremely relevant to the social and spiritual storm we find ourselves in right now in the United States.

- The maps no longer work.
- The bridges are destroyed.
- A status report is called for.
- Amazing acts of courage and bravery are discovered and lived out.
- A leadership vacuum is filled.
- An agenda for rebuilding is established.
- You replace the old structures with the new agenda.

Fast-forward to the twenty-first century. What followed the great escape birthed in the 1960s was a major trade-off. As previously discussed, the rank-and-file Christian left the major decision-making and policy-making arms of society in their rush to the marketplace, and a huge leadership vacuum was formed. In our search for the American Dream, we exchanged influence for the pursuit of affluence, and we gave up leadership positions to pursue a lifestyle that yearned for leisure.

But what happened in the wake of that monumental shift in our priorities was so much more than just a new trek or personal improvement. What resulted was moral, social, and spiritual surrender. Strong words? Yes. What did we surrender? Read on.

One of the critical lessons we have learned over the last forty-plus years is that we cannot "assume" anything about mankind other than what Scripture tells us. It says that our flesh desires the things of the flesh and not the things of the Spirit. That is our natural bent. The very reason many do not surrender their lives to Christ is that they simply want to be self-determining agents and to be the boss of their own lives. The mere thought of faith, or living by faith, is a frightening proposition for more people than one might think. A society left to the confines of the mortal mind leads to a world filled with the aftermath of a storm—a society bent on ridding itself of biblical, Christian influence. Think I'm wrong? Let's take a look at all that the church has surrendered over the past forty years.

In education, we have surrendered our collective voice in the curriculum, in the classroom, and in the decision-making process. Our curriculum now teaches evolution as the only viable explanation for our origins. In many states, the gay lifestyle and the homosexual agenda is at the forefront of the cultural sensitivity movement, while prayer and any reference to Scripture, including the Ten Commandments, have been removed entirely.

But the greatest loss suffered by the kingdom over the past forty-plus years has been in the halls of higher education—our nation's colleges and universities. You would be hard-pressed to find a substantial percentage of universities, secular or private, that do not openly mock our core beliefs and seek to debunk and strip each student of any Christian underpinnings or a Christian worldview. Objective examination of the subjects taught will show that our values have been exchanged for a socialist, secular agenda that has "lovingly" been labeled postmodern philosophy. While we have called it a secular worldview, its roots are embedded in failed regimes and failed societal models, mainly the European model that has resulted in social and moral anarchy, financial disaster, and a culture of terror and fear.

> The comfortable life is over for Christians in America.... We must be uncompromising in the insistence of our rights to worship and acknowledge Him as a free people not only in our thoughts but also in our actions. If we are truly Christian patriots...we must show that true love that ought to be characteristic of the Christian heart. This nation started out with a treasure trove of truth—the authority of the Word of God. We must be a reminder of the truths of that great treasure...so that once again our nation can be made whole on the basis of

that foundation…if it does not begin with us, that foundation will be permanently destroyed.[4]

—Dr. Alan Keyes
Former U.S. Ambassador to the UN Economic and Social Council

The tentacles of this tragic indoctrination are far-reaching and fatal, having a much greater impact here in the United States than you might have imagined. Consider this: there are four primary entities that literally determine the direction of this country—morally and otherwise. These four entities determine what is legal, what is probable, and what is true. These four entities are:

1. The legislative branch of the government
2. The judicial branch of the government
3. The secular scientific community
4. The church

Let's take a brief look at each of these entities so that you can understand why they literally determine the course of a nation—our nation—for good or bad.

The legislative branch of the government

The legislative branch of the U.S. government consists of the folks who make up the many law-making and policy-making entities all over the country—both state and federal. These men and women are elected officials who literally make the policies that we must live by as a nation. They decide if a woman can have a late-term abortion, if a homosexual couple can marry, the minimum wage, and whether or not a socially conservative or liberal judge sits on the Supreme Court.

The judicial branch of the government

Many believe that in the last twenty-five years, this branch of government has literally replaced the vote of the American people on initiatives, propositions, and the like, as they have the ability to uphold or strike down anything they deem to be inconsistent with their interpretation of the Constitution and the laws that have been established through the years. This group literally stands as the voice of right and wrong in the United States, interpreting laws and precedents set by previous cases. They determine matters related to everything from free speech, segregation, search and seizure, and admissions policies for universities. They regularly make decisions on the many moral issues that confront our nation.

The secular scientific community

This group of men and women get to decide what is plausible, what is true, and what is not. They get to interpret, explain, and determine the relevance of religious thought, discourse, and scientific evidence. They get to determine and tell the world the validity of the Bible and are allowed to go unchecked by scientific thought from scientists in the Christian community who believe contrary to their findings and agenda. The problem is, they are bound by a mandate to conduct all scientific endeavors absent the possibility of a creator or any kind of divine participation or intelligent design.

But the real problem is in the double standard that exists when they refuse to debate or examine scientific data and endeavors that allow for the possibility of an entity that over 85 percent of people in the United States believe is real—a God, a Creator. By discarding such scientific thought as irrelevant and not worthy of scientific inquiry or investigation, they violate one of the most sacred hallmarks of education: "Truth has nothing to fear from investigation."[5] Why can't the scientific community rally behind *that* thought and do the work of a scientist, examining all possibilities by using the same scientific method and critically examining the research done by their Christian colleagues who stand with their scientific evidence ready to have those discussions?

This is so critical to the discussion on the great escape by the church in that it used to be the Bible and its core truths that were taught as scientific fact and truth. The God of the Bible *was* the standard, completely without fear from investigation, knowing that whatever could not be proven scientifically in a particular era or year in history would soon be vindicated when scientific discovery caught up with the God of the

Bible. This one cost us a great deal of ground—ground that may not be reclaimed until every knee bows and every tongue confesses that Jesus is Lord. In the meantime, your children and mine must sit in public schools and be taught the theory of evolution as the most reasonable explanation for our origin. It's a theory without merit—not just scripturally, but scientifically—and time will prove it so. Our children will be forced to undertake every scientific experiment and learn mountains of scientific facts that are completely devoid of any participation or involvement by the very God they worship week in, week out. This one will cost us much.

The church

The church in the United States is the heart and soul of everything that is good and pure and moral. The church has always served to say to the rest of society, "This is God's mind on this or that," or "This is what God would have us do."

The problem is credibility. Whose church? Whose God? Whose Bible, and whose leaders do we listen to? We have so diluted and minimized our collective voice in the following four ways:

1. We cannot agree with each other.

2. We have stopped talking to the world and started talking almost exclusively to our own subculture of Christians.

3. Christianity is represented by the faces you see on television and the voices you hear on the radio airwaves. As long as the television faces keep falling, we will have serious credibility issues with the very culture we seek to win.

4. More and more messages are emerging that claim there are other "paths to God." The voice of the Muslim religion, Islam, and the intrigue that surrounds Eastern religions such as Buddhism have served to convolute an already convoluted message and to divide the religious base and its message, even when all espouse the same views on certain social issues. This, combined with media that glorify the

divide and recognize all as equally valid while marginalizing the Christian right, makes for a lethal concoction of impotence. This renders the voice of the one true God irrelevant and out of touch with the ways of man.

In short, people have exchanged the truth for a lie, and by our silence, we have let them once again fill our void. One of the ways this has happened is with the closest cousin we have—conservative talk radio. Once again, we have left the fight to the generals and have stopped speaking out, exchanging participation for hour after hour of cheering on Shawn Hannity, Rush Limbaugh, Bill O'Reilly, and their contemporaries.

Problem is, these superstar conservatives may espouse a conservative agenda to perfection and never win one soul to Christ. We must never forget that God is neither Republican nor Democrat and politics is not tops on His agenda. We are called to be so much more, and our silence in the arena of public discourse is deafening.

THE AFTERMATH OF A STORM

Chuck Colson, in his book titled *Developing a Christian Worldview of the Problem of Evil*, states: "When we close our eyes to the human capacity for evil, we fail to build the moral boundaries needed to protect us from that evil."[6] In a recent study by the RAND Corporation titled "Watching Sex on Television Predicts Adolescent Initiation of Sexual Behavior," their research found:

- Sixty-four percent of all television programs contain sexual content.

- Those programs that contain sexual content average 4.4 scenes per hour with sexually related material.

- Forty-six percent of high school students in the United States have had sexual intercourse.

- Each year, one case of a sexually transmitted disease (STD) is diagnosed for every four sexually active teens in the United States.

- The rate of teen pregnancy in the United States is among the highest of all industrialized countries.

- The average youth watches three hours of television daily, and sexual messages are commonplace.

- Approximately one of every seven programs includes a portrayal of sexual intercourse, depicted or strongly implied.

And here are a few of the clinchers:

- Television may create the illusion that sex is more central to daily life than it truly is and may promote sexual initiation as a result, a process known as media cultivation.

- Youths in the ninetieth percentile of viewing sex on television had a predicted probability of intercourse that was approximately double that of youths in the tenth percentile.

- And, sadly "although intercourse among youths is common (46 percent), most sexually active teens say they wish they had waited longer to have sex."[7]

It is my observation that a very interesting phenomenon is occurring in the television and motion-picture industries of America. It is my belief that media in this country, especially television and film, no longer reflect the mood, the moral direction, or the daily life of the people they claim to portray. I believe that the opposite is in fact the case. Television and films are now being created to dictate the mood, create the morals, and dictate the daily life of the people of this country. One example of this would be a recent article in *USA Today* that found that "about half of Americans over age 18 are married, but [only] 18.1 percent of major movie characters are."[8]

Additionally, the number of sexual relationships outside the boundary of marriage is extremely high. Add to that the fact that we as Christians, while being an enormous percentage of the population in the United States, are basically absent from all television shows and movies, as is church attendance, prayer, and any consideration for spiritual discernment in decision making. This is not only appalling but also grossly inaccurate and completely *not* representative of the people in this country. How about in the church?

> A new study from the Barna Research Group of Ventura, California, shows that millions of twentysomething Americans—many of whom were active in churches during their teens—pass through their most formative adult decade while putting Christianity on the back burner. The research, conducted with 2,660 twentysomethings, shows that Americans in their twenties are significantly less likely than any other age group to attend church services, to donate to churches, to be absolutely committed to Christianity, to read the Bible, or to serve as a volunteer or lay leader in churches.[9]

One of the greatest concerns we should all share for the evangelical church in the United States is that, according to the Barna Research Group, 80 percent of people who regularly attended church in their teens will leave the church by age twenty-nine if something the shape and size of a revolution does not occur soon.[10]

One Hundred Inches of Rain

The maps no longer work, the bridges have been destroyed, and a status report is called for. Amazing acts of courage and bravery must be discovered and lived out. A leadership vacuum must be filled. An agenda for rebuilding must be established, and we must replace the existing social structures with the new agenda—one that carries the voice of the Creator of the universe—while we are still allowed to have a voice at all.

> If you put the U.S. up against the Scriptures, we're in trouble. I think we are very close to the judgment of God. The problem of America is not the unbelieving world. The problem of America is the people of God.

Right now, there are just as many divorces in the churches as there are outside the churches. There are just as many abortions, and there's only a one percent difference in gambling inside the churches as outside the churches. It's God's people who hold the destiny of America. Don't fuss at the world. It's acting just like its nature. We've got to be salt and light again. We've got to have an observable difference.[11]

—Henry Blackaby

SECTION 6

FALL IN

A religion that offers its sons to die in fiery suicide bomb attacks will only be penetrated by a gospel whose adherents are more willing to die as martyrs at the hands of their persecutors than take up the sword in defense of their faith. "Guns and bombs will not change the Muslim world, but the gospel will," explains Brother Yun. "Perhaps thousands of Chinese missionaries will die in the evangelization of the Muslim world."[1]

—*Ministry Today*

HOLY DISCONTENT

The growing movement of Christian revolutionaries in the U.S. distinguished themselves from an already-select group of people—born-again Christians—through their deeds, beliefs and self-views. Revolutionaries demonstrated substantially higher levels of community service, financial contributions, daily Bible study, personal quiet times each day, family Bible studies, daily worship experiences, engagement in spiritual mentoring, and evangelistic efforts. They also had a series of beliefs that were much more likely than those of typical born again adults to coincide with biblical teachings. Their self-perceptions were also dramatically different than that of other born again adults.[1]

—Barna Research Group

I GREW UP IN THE HIGH-DESERT REGION OF SOUTHERN CALIFORNIA in a place called Antelope Valley. I never saw an antelope, but I'd see jackrabbits and coyotes from time to time. While I loved my growing-up years and have many fond memories, I absolutely did *not* like living in the desert. It was always windy. The summer months were extremely hot (100–110 degrees), and dust blew all over the place. This is particularly bad since I am allergic to dust. Everything was brown, which meant everything was either dead or dying. *Ugh!* So when I got the opportunity to move out of the valley as a college student, I thought I had died and gone to heaven.

I did my undergraduate work in Orange County, California, which I firmly believe is one of the most beautiful places on the planet. It is absolutely beautiful year-round, and the ocean is never more than a short drive away. Everything is green all the time, and there is seldom any notable wind! I spent nearly sixteen years living in OC before moving to Georgia.

In the last several years that I lived in Orange County, I was struck by the number of church plants that popped up all over the place. It seemed like there was a new church plant on every corner, in all the schools, meeting at different kinds of hours if necessary, and with all different kinds of names. The names were so inventive, it seemed as if they were birthed out of a pioneering-type spirit. Each new church plant was seeking to break the mold and venture into new territory, or so it seemed until I noticed another phenomenon. It seemed that these dozens upon dozens of church plants would each be around for a year or two, and then they'd be gone, vanished, or under new management by a new church plant with an improved, modernized name. That new church would be gone as well in short order.

For a variety of reasons, I was able to meet some of these church planters. They were adventuresome souls bent on making a mark in the kingdom. As I began to meet some of these well-meaning folks, I made a few discoveries. Now, I realize that this may upset some of you, but you can hear it and test your motives by it or just get offended and stomp off. The fact is that 32 percent of all new church plants close their doors within four years.[2] Why? Why is that the case? Well, I actually have several theories about that, and most would offend, but what I will say is this: I am always amazed that so many people felt called to Orange County, one of the most beautiful places on the earth, to start a church or to birth a ministry. Actually, the more I watched this happen, the more it became abundantly clear to me that the real reason they chose Orange County to do their church plant was that they either lived there already or wanted to live there in the worst way. Who wouldn't?

Now, this is not a commentary on starting churches in Orange County or on church planting at all. In fact, there is a great need for new churches in parts of Orange County, especially churches that are able to reach across cultural, language, and color boundaries as this is now one of the most diverse counties in the country. What I am saying is that while our intentions may be good, our thinking may be all wrong. To think that we can select the field we are to harvest based on our personal preferences for a particular quality of life and standard of living is flawed thinking. That is *not* the way of the cross and is everything that the story of the rich young ruler seeks to teach us. We must think bigger, and we must submit our calling to the authority and the leading of the God of the universe.

For far too many years, our churches have produced individuals who become inspired, have an idea, or want to do their own thing. They run off to do something amazing for God while asking Him to bless it as they go. They leap, and then they pray. They fall down, and then they pray harder. Then no rescue comes, so they stay down, disillusioned, bitter, and disenfranchised, all the while surrounded by those who went with them and who are asking, "What do we do now?"

FALL IN

To fall in means simply to get in line with the rest of the company and await your orders from the throne. It is a military term, and it means to assemble with the rest of the troops, to be a part of a mission that we are all involved in together. Can you imagine what would happen if we went to war and every soldier just got off the plane, each with his or her own idea about how to win the war, and then each went off on their own separate way, bent on victory their way? Some would form groups, some would follow a charismatic leader, and while there would be thousands of soldiers on the ground, each would be doing what was right in his or her own eyes. No central command, no one giving orders—or, should I say, no one *taking* orders; that might be a better parallel. Can you imagine it?

Well, you don't have to imagine any longer. I just described much of the church in the twenty-first century. Christians are at war against a very real enemy, and there are far too many of us out doing our own thing for God. We are outside the covering of a church and outside the covering of any spiritual authority whatsoever, and it is hurting the overall effort. Meanwhile, hundreds of well-meaning soldiers and even warriors for Christ are experiencing defeat.

The real problem goes right back to the core message of this book: all paths to your purpose, your destiny, and your mission on Earth lead through relationship with Christ. There are no shortcuts—none. You simply will not hear the voice of God absent a living, breathing, walking, and talking daily relationship with Him. While many of you are down with the prayer thing, the Bible-study thing, the worship thing, and even the giving thing, too many of us struggle with the church thing or the connecting-with-other-believers thing.

Far too many of us have witnessed firsthand the abuse, neglect, and hurt that can come at the hands of flesh-and-blood men and women in pastoral or leadership roles. Some—far too many—have said, "No way. I'll do it myself, my way." Problem is, "my way" will never be God's plan for any life. His way leads through the church, His very bride; far too many 501(c)(3)s and other noble efforts to serve God have strayed outside the covering of the army of God and have become *mercenaries*—not *missionaries*—for God.

Falling in requires surrender. Problem is, that could mean anywhere, anytime, and at any cost. Now we are right back to the analogy of the rich young ruler. To *surrender* means to become a part of God's activity alongside others He has called to His plan in a particular area, and far too many of us simply do not play well with others. That is known by its real name: pride.

It's easy to live in plush places and have the best schools, the best weather, the cleanest streets, and the greatest amount of recreational opportunities afforded to man, but perhaps God has a different mission for you. What do you do with that?

> It is one of God's recurring dreams to raise up servants intent upon reaching those who have been impoverished materially, spiritually and emotionally—those people who have been forgotten, abused and rejected. There are many churches and missional movements that began with fiery passion, founded by wild-eyed youth, to minister to such neglected communities as coal miners or street kids. But visionary Christian movements to the world's margins have been born and subsequently died dozens of times through the ages. Some of the idealistic fervor of revolutionary movements has been lost in

many quarters of the church today, overshadowed by an obsession with self-improvement and accumulation, and an acquiescence to the shopping mall mentality.[3]

—Scott Bessenecker

Are you a soldier in the army of God or a mercenary who will take orders from no one? Are you willing to let God use you in a radical way? Will you use every fiber of your created being to carry out a mission that is just for you yet part of the overall plan? Are you willing to come under the authority of a church and submit your agenda to the commander in chief, even if all you get in return is one year parking cars or changing diapers? Are you willing to do that? Are you willing to fall in and wait to see what God wants you to do and then do it?

I keep thinking back to my close friend who knew exactly what he wanted to do for God but ignored ministry opportunities that kept knocking at his door. Nothing was going right in the ministry of his choosing, and everyone could see what a natural fit he was for ministering to all of the men who had lost their children—everyone, that is, but him. How sad for him and for those men.

Now, let's get back to one of the most foundational truths for Christians seeking their calling today: what you want to do for God may not be what He wants you to do for Him. If all you are doing is trying to make your square peg fit into that round hole, you will find yourself frustrated, confused, disoriented, and eventually bitter. There may be a round peg sitting right there, begging you to pick it up. There are far too many churches filled with frustrated, confused, disoriented, bitter folks. They are not hard to spot. They are usually the most defensive, negative, and sometimes even manipulative people in the church. My pastor refers to these folks as "cranctified" saints (as opposed to sanctified saints). These folks don't need more meetings and more change; they need more discernment and more spiritual sensitivity. These folks love the Lord and just want to serve Him, but many are blinded to their own strengths and weaknesses, and sometimes the truth spoken in love is better than a thousand false compliments.

God absolutely has an incredible plan for you, and in the next few chapters, I believe you will find something that makes your heart jump and your lips say, "That's it!" God is doing something new in the earth today through His people. The roads are gone, and the bridges are out—all that's true. God is using new roads and building new bridges to the lost, and that's where we come in. I cannot wait to show you the grass-roots uprising the Lord is in the process of planting and developing, and I can't wait to help you see your role in this revolution. The battle is there, absolutely, but it is ours for the winning if each of us will simply fall in and await the specifics of our mission.

> Jesus did not have to dream up what He could do for the Father. He watched to see what the Father was doing around His life, and Jesus put His life there. The Father then could accomplish His purposes through Jesus. This is exactly what Jesus wants us to do with His lordship in our lives. We see what He is doing, and adjust our lives, our plans, and our goals to Him. We are to place our lives at His disposal—where he is working—so He can accomplish His purposes through us.[4]
>
> —Henry Blackaby

chapter 23

THE BATTLE FOR
THE MIND OF MAN

As you come to him, the living Stone—rejected by men but chosen
by God and precious to him—you also, like living stones, are
being built into a spiritual house to be a holy priesthood, offering
spiritual sacrifices acceptable to God through Jesus Christ…But
you are a chosen people, a royal priesthood, a holy nation, a people
belonging to God, that you may declare the praises of him who
called you out of darkness into his wonderful light. Once you
were not a people, but now you are the people of God; once you
had not received mercy, but now you have received mercy.
                                        —1 Peter 2:4–5, 9–10, NIV

E VERY WAR HAS BATTLE PLANS. SOME ARE COMPLEX, AND SOME ARE
simple, but there is always a battle plan. Knowing that the struggle
in this battle is for the mind of man and for the children of man,
I began to examine over the last forty to fifty years a few different battle plans,
or strategies that have been used for reaching the mind of man and the children of man. If you are keeping score, the Christian church is losing ground
at a rapid pace.

> Most Americans have a period of time during their teen years when
> they are actively engaged in a church youth group. However, Barna's
> tracking of young people showed that most of them had disengaged
> from organized religion during their twenties.[1]

So, the odds for our victory don't look so good with physical eyes, and the
stats we hear don't sound so good with physical ears. Any way you look at it,

we need to take a good, hard look at what is happening and where we have been in order to chart a path forward.

Here are a few examples of growth strategies of a few major religious movements over the last fifty years:

Catholic church

- Baby baptism
- No contraception
- Quality Catholic schools
- Confirmation
- Strong community through parishes
- Greater freedom with social issues

Mormon church

- Generational growth through very large families
- Social relevance
- Financial stability in each home
- Strong focus on family and children
- Strong focus on teen culture and activities
- Strong focus on religious education for youth

New Age church

- Freedom of movement and freedom from judgment
- Appeals to the senses
- Appeals to the logic (mind) of man
- Strong attachment to nature and the aesthetic side of man
- Allows the individual to be in control of their own destiny
- Powerful feelings and intense emotion using all of the five senses
- Movie stars as role models and spokespersons

Eastern religions

- Very similar to the New Age movement
- Promised enlightenment, which makes you better and smarter
- Beautiful symbols and cultural appeal
- Peaceful and nonthreatening approach
- Places higher value on logic than on dependence on God
- Promotes control of your own destiny
- Appeals to the five senses
- Movie stars as role models

Evangelical church

- Church planting
- Missions
- Crusades and revivals
- Visitation
- Youth ministries
- Children's ministries
- Bible education through discipleship and Sunday school

Now, here is what I want you to see that I believe is so incredibly astounding. Satan has had a strategy for over forty years to capture the mind of man and the children of man. It is methodical, it is patient, it is all-encompassing, it is ever evolving, and it is brilliant. If we were keeping score, he would appear to be way ahead with only a few innings left to play.

SATAN'S PLAN

Abortion on demand

Adult bookstores

Adult counselors for abortion

Alcohol

Anger

Anorexia

Bulimia

Child abuse

Childhood obesity

Corruption in high places

Credit card industry

Daytime television

Desensitization

Drugs

Fallen pastors/preachers

False religions

Famous people

Fashion

Fear

Foster care

Free clinics to obtain contraception

Free condoms

Gangs

Hate

Homosexuality

Hotel room television

iPods

Jewelry

Liberal judges

Liberal lawmakers

Low self-esteem

Magazines

Many senators and congresspersons

Monetary wealth

Most universities

Movies

Music

Newspapers

Nightclubs

No parental notification of abortion

No-fault divorce

Numerical superiority

Organized crime

Orphanages

Pay-per-view television

Pornography

Portable media players

Poverty

Preoccupation with skin color

Prime-time television

Prisons

The psychological community

Revisionist history

Role models

The scientific community

Separation of church and state

Sex

Sex education

Strip clubs

Superior courts

Television news

Terrorism

Values training in schools

Video games

Violence

Violence in movies

Virtual reality games and lifestyles

I have just listed sixty-seven paths—sixty-seven bridges—that Satan has constructed and traveled for some fifty to sixty years now that have resulted in one hundred inches of rain, devastation, and tragedy. He knows where these folks are. He knows their appetites, and he's got the bait. The pornography industry is at an all-time high, and church plants are down. Eastern and Middle Eastern religions are up. Our numbers are shrinking. We have to realize that this is war and that we had better come together on this, or it will be our kids they come for, our kids they win. This is not just some persecuted pastor on another continent that we can simply ignore and turn a blind eye to. It's here. It's real, and it's playing for keeps.

So strong is this new world that evil has wrought that we in the church had better pay attention to two very important trends that have emerged. We have two very significant windows of opportunity for victory in people's lives that we had better capitalize on soon. *We must get them before they fall in to the clutches of sin and death, and we must wait with open arms and a plan when they surface just long enough to gasp for air and reach for a lifeline.*

I have always heard it said that if people do not accept Christ by the age of eighteen, 80 percent never will. Barna's research says it is even more critical than that. A person's views related to God and religion are pretty much decided by age twelve, and there is very little, if any, change in those views for the rest of their lives—for most folks. We better win them while they are young, whatever the cost, whatever the price.[2]

A WAVE OF OPPORTUNITY

The strategy of Satan is indeed those sixty-seven paths I noted, and a whole lot more. But as Christians and as students of the times, we all know that nearly all of those paths lead to destruction, death, and devastation. I prophetically proclaim that our churches will be lighthouses to the devastated, the hopeless, and the defeated and that they will come in droves to our doorsteps, seeking hope, help, and a new life. They will bring their children in tow, and they won't know much, if anything, about our ways, our customs, or our way of life. How we respond to these folks, this "multitude in the valley of decision," will be the difference between a catastrophe or a harvest. It will be a catastrophe if we are not prepared and a harvest if we have a plan and our people receive them as if they had been waiting for years for them to arrive. They won't look like us, they won't act like us, and they won't know what to do. They will only know they are compelled to come and see if there is any hope for them at all this side of the grave.

We had better be prepared for God to do a new thing in our midst, and we had better be ready for the children because they are coming. We had better be ready for the newly divorced, the girl who has had an abortion, the man who has just lost his family, the adulterous woman who wants to end her sinful existence but does not know how or who to tell, and the man or woman fresh out of jail or in need of rehabilitation.

> As Jesus passed from there, He saw a man named Matthew sitting at the tax office. And He said to him, "Follow Me." So he arose and followed Him. Now it happened, as Jesus sat at the table in the house, that behold, many tax collectors and sinners came and sat down with Him and His disciples. And when the Pharisees saw it, they said to His disciples, "Why does your Teacher eat with tax collectors and sinners?" When Jesus heard that, He said to them, "Those who are well have no need of a physician, but those who are sick. But go and learn what this means: 'I desire mercy and not sacrifice.' For I did not come to call the righteous, but sinners, to repentance."
>
> —Matthew 9:9–13

I believe there is a way to go where the bridges used to go. In fact, there are many revolutionaries who are already there, but they are few against multitudes, and reinforcements are desperately needed. There is a plan. I have seen it, and in the next few chapters, I will unveil it to you. It is a powerful plan. It is a God-given plan, and there is a place for you in the battle for Planet Earth. You may think you are not qualified, and by that very admission you just became qualified. God is not looking for your ability as much as He is looking for your availability. God's plan is to use ordinary people—His people—in extraordinary ways so that when all is said and done, the glory goes to God, not man—not you, and not me. That is a plan for victory no matter how great the odds.

chapter 24

THE PLAN—OPERATION: RESCUE THE PERISHING

"Do not fear what they fear; do not be frightened." But in your hearts set apart Christ as Lord. Always be prepared to give an answer to everyone who asks You to give the reason for the hope that you have. But do this with gentleness and respect.

—1 Peter 3:14–15, NIV

L ET'S TAKE A LOOK AT WHAT WE KNOW. THE ENEMY IS AMONG US, and we have surrendered valuable ground. We have lost our universities; most state and federal legislatures; most supreme courts; and numerous major court decisions, including the most famous, *Roe v. Wade.* Homosexuality is being pushed upon society and our children, demanding acceptance and equal status with marriage between a man and a woman. Drugs, alcohol, and tobacco have claimed hundreds of thousands of lives, and our churches are in decline numerically.[1]

But we also know that God is still on the throne, and He is not surprised or caught off guard. He is moving and stirring up His people to ready them for a battle similar to the Revolutionary War. Only this war is of a spiritual nature with more at stake than the future of a nation—multitudes, multitudes in the valley of decision.

There is a great scene in the movie *The Patriot* where you can see the war beginning between the English and the newly formed patriots, and the good guys are getting slaughtered. Mel Gibson stands in his living room when he makes this profound statement: "It's a slaughter out there. We can't win fighting them their way" (paraphrased). New day, but same truth. We cannot overcome corruption with tougher policing. We cannot defeat immorality with more laws. More medicine will not stop the spread of disease, and more money alone will not stop poverty. The same goes for our battle with principalities and against the powers in high places. We cannot defeat evil with swords and guns. So what's the plan? Are you ready for this? Here it is:

THE FIVE-PRONGED BATTLE PLAN

1. Embrace the hour in which we live.

I believe I have made the case for the hour in which we live both prophetically in Scripture as well as socially being ripe for God's judgment. It appears a perfect storm is brewing. Scripture talks about this time, but it also talks about an outpouring of God's Spirit like never before. These are not days to go weak in the knees or to bury your head in the sand. These may be the most incredibly exciting and profound years in the history of the church. Embrace that, get all the way in, and find your place on the wall.

The most important thing to remember about the hour in which we live is that *the fields are riper than they appear and more accessible than previously imagined.* Throughout the years, I have witnessed again and again men and women who many thought never would budge come to Christ. I have seen the aged and the hard-core sinner bow their knee to Christ, and then I watched them months later raise their hands in the air with tears in their eyes, worshiping God as if they had been doing so for years. We underestimate our God and the power of the cross.

Many years ago, farmers in the Show-Me State of Missouri found that they could actually farm land that they had previously thought was unreachable because of the rivers that ran through the land. They spent decades looking across the rivers at beautiful, fertile ground, thinking it was no use to even try to farm it. Someone discovered that the river had places that were crossable, and—*voilà!*—they were now able to farm land they never thought was even reachable. It's the same with people today, the unreachable people.

I believe that over the next several years, we are going to see very prominent people come to Christ simply because we begin to try. We are so quick to write off politicians, movie stars, athletes, and musicians as unreachable and not worth the effort. We make the assumption that they have sin that even God can't forgive. We think that they are above religion and above the message of the gospel, but nothing could be further from the truth.

2. Our weapons are not carnal.

While there are and will be wars and rumors of wars, our weapons are spiritual in nature. Our weapons are love, mercy, hope, compassion, grace, purpose, and salvation. Souls—not land and political power—are the trophies of war.

3. Every man and every woman has a post with orders from the throne.

If there is one mistake we have made more than once throughout the centuries, it is putting too much responsibility for the health and the stealth of the church on the shoulders of its generals. It's time we put ourselves on call for an all-out grassroots effort. (More on the grassroots effort in the next chapter.) There is a place for you in this battle, and chances are that place of service is both something the Lord has been doing in you for some time now and something that looks a lot like the things that you were born to do. God is going to do a new thing on the earth, and He is going to do it through His people, the church—through you!

> Who then is Paul, and who is Apollos, but ministers through whom you believed, as the Lord gave to each one? I planted, Apollos watered, but God gave the increase. So then neither he who plants is anything, nor he who waters, but God who gives the increase. Now he who plants and he who waters are one, and each will receive his own reward according to his own labor. For we are God's fellow workers; you are God's field, you are God's building. According to the grace of God which was given to me, as a wise master builder I have laid the foundation, and another builds on it. But let each one take heed how he builds on it. For no other foundation can anyone lay than that which is laid, which is Jesus Christ.
>
> —1 Corinthians 3:5–11

4. We must win the war at home.

Every day, every way, every hour of every day, we absolutely have to win the war at home. Our faith must be passed on to the next generation. Passing on godly heritage to your child is the most important thing you can do for your children. One of the greatest weapons in Satan's arsenal is that of distraction. Distraction can divert attention away from the home, leaving it vulnerable to the attacks of the enemy. Pay attention. Spend time with each member of your family. Establish routine traditions and standards that are immovable—all couched in arms that constantly extend love, acceptance, and care.

5. We do not war alone; all of heaven stands by our side.

Hebrews chapter 12 gives an incredible picture of a stadium full of the heroes of the Bible, cheering us on from the bleachers. They have walked where we have walked and have that twenty-twenty hindsight perspective on life as they knew it, with all of its timeless truths.

> Therefore we also, since we are surrounded by so great a cloud of witnesses, let us lay aside every weight, and the sin that so easily ensnares us, and let us run with endurance the race that is set before us.
> —Hebrews 12:1

One of my favorite Bible stories is found in the Old Testament, and it paints the perfect picture of what is true for every believer in every dark hour, trial, or battle.

> Therefore the heart of the king of Syria was greatly troubled by this thing; and he called his servants and said to them, "Will you not show me which of us is for the king of Israel?" And one of his servants said, "None, my lord, O king; but Elisha, the prophet who is in Israel, tells the king of Israel the words that you speak in your bedroom." So he said, "Go and see where he is, that I may send and get him." And it was told him, saying, "Surely he is in Dothan." Therefore he sent horses and chariots and a great army there, and they came by night and surrounded

the city. And when the servant of the man of God [Elisha] arose early and went out, there was an army, surrounding the city with hoses and chariots. And his servant said to him, "Alas, my master! What shall we do?" So he [Elisha] answered, "Do not fear, for those who are with us are more than those who are with them." And Elisha prayed, and said, "LORD, I pray, open his eyes that he may see." Then the LORD opened the eyes of the young man, and he saw. And behold, the mountain was full of horses and chariots of fire all around Elisha.

—2 Kings 6:11–17

Man, I love that story! It paints the picture for what is true for you and for me as we walk bravely into war and as we traverse behind enemy lines. We do not go alone, and us plus the army of God are pretty good odds, but notice that the servant's physical eyes could not see what was true, and neither will yours.

If you read history you will find that the Christians who did most for the present world were precisely those who thought most of the next. It is since Christians have largely ceased to think of the other world that they have become so ineffective in this [world].[2]

—C. S. Lewis

chapter 25

FINDING YOUR VOICE—THE
GRASSROOTS REVOLUTION

One of the things I tell men is this: Don't ask yourself what
the world needs. Ask yourself what makes you come alive
and do that. Because what the world needs are men who
have come alive.[1]

—John Eldredge

LET ME ASK YOU SOME QUESTIONS: WHO ARE YOU REALLY? WHAT
drives and motivates you? What do you love to do? Better yet, what are
your greatest strengths? I believe with every fiber of my being that we
are missing it big-time in too many U.S. churches. We have not allowed for the
possibility that God could be doing a new thing in the earth. One of my abso-
lute favorite speakers is Erwin McManus. He says, "Creativity is the natural
result of spirituality."[2] One of the characteristics of the outpouring is dreams,
visions, and prophecy (Joel 2:28) and with that, I believe, comes a new move of
God through His people.

Where do you fit in? What do you do with all the Lord is showing
you? By now, I pray that you are doing the stuff that makes for a living,
breathing, walking, and talking relationship with Christ. As such, you
have done the work of purification and have pushed through the key quit-
ting points and find yourself here today, saying, "I'm in!" What comes
next is to find your place on the wall, your mission and your purpose for
such a time as this. I want to show you a glimpse of what God might be
doing in you and through you and help bring you closer to your role in all
of this, your calling.

First, let me ask you ten purpose-focused questions that have been very helpful to others through the years. Think about each question for a moment, and then write down your answers:

1. What would you attempt to do if you knew you could not fail?

2. What would you do for free if you could do it well?

3. If you could pick one area of your life where you would like to see God working in greater ways, where would it be?

4. If you were given ten million dollars, how would you use it, and what charities and/or causes would you most likely contribute to?

5. Who is living your dream, and what, specifically, are they doing?

6. What kinds of things do you do best?

7. What do others give you the most positive feedback for?

8. Who do you have a passion to help the most?

9. What do you want others to say about you at your funeral?

10. When all is said and done, what do you want God to say about you?

Here are two key points to go along with the questions above: (1) Who you are beneath the surface is who you're supposed to be and the life you're supposed to lead; and, (2) what God has for you to do is probably a continuation of what He has been doing in you all along.

> God works in sequence to accomplish his divine purposes. What he did in the past was done with a Kingdom purpose in mind. What he is doing in the present is in sequence with the past and with the same kingdom purpose in mind. Every act of God builds on the past with a view toward the future.[3]
>
> —Henry Blackaby

Now, let me show you something that may knock your socks off! There is a stirring in the people of God, a "holy discontent." The children of God are becoming keenly aware that there is more—another level—and they want it. They are discerning that evil is in our midst, and they are standing ready to fight. They want to be a part of something that is real, and they want to do more than just go to church.

If that sounds like you, I have something very profound for you to consider. As I prayed that the Lord would show me more about what this grassroots effort would look like, I believe that I received a revelation of great magnitude. The Lord took me back to Satan's strategy for *the mind of man* and the *children of man*.

As I began to look at that list, a light went on in my head. I no longer saw sixty-seven strategies that Satan used over the last fifty to sixty years. Instead, I saw bridges, roads, and strongholds of the enemy with many souls held captive in each of those strongholds. This leads me to challenge you to do the following: look over this list again, and see if you don't see for yourself a mission field that makes your heart leap, skip a beat, and yearn for a God-sized mission. These are the areas where Christian men and women could infiltrate and take ground.

NEW ROADS AND NEW BRIDGES

Abortion on demand	Daytime television
Adult bookstores	Desensitization
Adult counselors for abortion	Drugs
Alcohol	Fallen pastors/preachers
Anger	False religions
Anorexia	Famous people
Bulimia	Fashion
Child abuse	Fear
Childhood obesity	Foster care
Corruption in high places	Free clinics to obtain contraception
Credit card industry	Free condoms

Gangs
Hate
Homosexuality
Hotel room television
iPods
Jewelry
Liberal judges
Liberal lawmakers
Low self-esteem
Magazines
Many senators and congresspersons
Monetary wealth
Most universities
Movies
Music
Newspapers
Nightclubs
No parental notification of abortion
No-fault divorce
Numerical superiority
Organized crime
Orphanages
Pay-per-view television

Pornography
Portable media players
Poverty
Preoccupation with skin color
Prime-time television
Prisons
The psychological community
Revisionist history
Role models
The scientific community
Separation of church and state
Sex
Sex education
Strip clubs
Superior courts
Television news
Terrorism
Values training in schools
Video games
Violence
Violence in movies
Virtual reality games and lifestyles

For far too long, we have looked at serving God through this narrow scope of the few full-time vocations the ministry affords, or the many different functions a church needs to function. In that narrow view, far too many do not see a place for them. Well, this list of sixty-seven areas of influence hold many ministry opportunities, mission fields, and ways to invest in a life and to rescue the perishing.

It is important to always remember that *wherever you are, God,* light, and hope are within reach. Did you see yourself in any of these areas? I believe that the Lord is going to raise up men and women to invade and even take back territory that has been lost to Satan.

Matthew Barnett is the son of a very famous pastor named Tommy Barnett. While it is common to see Tommy's name all across the country in conferences, television programs, and retreats, you will not find Matthew's name out there on the circuit so much—at least not yet. Matthew has taken one of those new roads to the lost and is building a new bridge that leads to some of the toughest neighborhoods in America. Matthew had a dream at a very young age to reach one of the most unreachable cities in the world: Los Angeles, California. Many veterans of the war told him not to go there, not to get his hopes up, and that he would be in grave danger if he went. All Matthew knew was that God said to go.

Matthew is a good friend of my home church, and we have had the privilege of hosting Matthew to speak at a few events. His stories are always amazing. He told us one about the time he spoke at his home church when he was very young. Through a cracked-open door, he heard some of the old guard talking, men he respected very much. He heard them say, "Well, his daddy sure has it, but, the poor boy, he just don't have it." This devastated him but served to drive him to the very place God needed him to be so he could see another way, another road, and another bridge.

But the story I love most is the story of his early days trying to start a church in Los Angeles.

Matthew talks about going there to start a church with eighteen people, but one Sunday, only two showed up. It was then that Matthew had his next-level encounter and began to build a church unlike any other. He simply began meeting people's needs with a radical, hands-on gospel. He began to see that there were spirit people beneath the rough exterior, and he began to sense that God was about to do a new thing in a place everyone said was unreachable, and reach them he did. They now minister to over forty thousand people each week and have over eight thousand in their weekly Sunday morning services. This new thing is called the Dream Center, and it is located in Los Angeles, California. They house, feed, rehabilitate, and minister in such a way that the crime has dropped by large percentages in their neighborhood for the third straight year.

Did Matthew do something no one else could do, or did he simply join God in what He was about to do the same way you can? Which is it? I firmly believe that if you are walking in the light in daily relationship with Christ and if you have surrendered your will and your agenda to the King of kings, then He will show you what He is up to that He wants you to be a part of. The rest is just a matter of submission, availability, courage, and obedience.

I believe with all my heart and with all of my mind that the army God is assembling will look less and less like the traditional church and more and more like a mosaic of movements, incursions, and holy insurgencies into enemy territory in the ultimate rescue mission that goes deep into the valley of decision.

God is moving, and if you will be sensitive to His Spirit, your spirit will begin to stir within you, and He will show you things and reveal to you your role in His incredible plan. When you begin to understand all that God is up to and all of the ways that He is moving, the following passages of Scripture begin to take on new meaning with greater implication for your life.

> For I know the thoughts that I think toward you, says the LORD, thoughts of peace and not of evil, to give you a future and a hope. Then you will call upon Me and go and pray to Me, and I will listen to you. And you will seek Me and find Me, when you search for Me with all your heart. I will be found by you, says the LORD, and I will bring you back from your captivity.
>
> —Jeremiah 29:11–14

> Who, then, is the man that fears the LORD?
>> He will instruct him in the way chosen for him.
> He will spend his days in prosperity,
>> and his descendants will inherit the land.
> The LORD confides in those who fear him;
>> he makes his covenant known to them.
>
> —Psalm 25:12–14, NIV

George Barna is right. There is a revolution brewing, and like the revolution that birthed this great nation, God is raising an army of regular folks to do incredible feats of bravery and innovation. The enemy is among us, and his allies are marching from the north, the south, and certainly the east. We are in the West, but we no longer speak for the West—not like we once did—but it is God's voice that still rules over all, and He is calling to the army of the Almighty: "Fall in!"

> You need to overcome the tug of people against you as you reach for high goals.... All men are afraid in battle. The coward is the one who lets fear overcome his sense of duty.[4]
>
> —George Patton

chapter 26

FINDING *OUR* VOICE

The LORD your God himself will drive them out of your way.
He will push them out before you, and you will take possession
of their land, as the LORD your God promised you. Be very
strong; be careful to obey all that is written in the Book of
the Law of Moses, without turning aside to the right or the
left. Do not associate with these nations that remain among
you; do not invoke the names of their gods or swear by them.
You must not serve them or bow down to them. But you are
to hold fast to the LORD your God, as you have until now. The
LORD has driven out before you great and powerful nations;
to this day no one has been able to withstand you. One of
you routs a thousand, because the LORD your God fights for
you, just as he promised. So be very careful to love the LORD
your God.

—Joshua 23:5–11, NIV

A MOVE OF GOD HAS HAD MANY NAMES THROUGHOUT THE YEARS.
Billy Graham called it a crusade, and many in my childhood referred
to it as a revival. Modern-day leaders have also given names to the
movement of God in our day. Erwin McManus calls it an uprising; George
Barna calls it a revolution. The Book of Revelation calls it a harvest, and the
Book of Joel calls it an outpouring. Joel also talks about the latter rain, speaking
directly to the outpouring of the Spirit of God on His church, saying: "And it
shall come to pass afterward [which most Bible scholars believe refers to the
time period just before the return of Christ] that I will pour out My Spirit
on all flesh; your sons and your daughters shall prophesy, your old men shall

dream dreams, your young men shall see visions. And also on My menservants and My maidservants, I will pour out My Spirit in those days" (Joel 2:28–29).

Call it anything you like, but know this: God is on the move, and He is going to use the millions of pew-sitting men and women of God to wage a grassroots revolution. This uprising will cause most of America's pastors to rise up and lead as they have never led before.

On the page that follows, I want to walk you through all that God is doing in the earth today. His plan is to reach the unreachable valleys and the seemingly impenetrable fortresses of the evil one by using new roads, building newer bridges, and possessing weapons designed expressly for such an assault.

Reaching the lost with:

1. Salvation	
2. A plan for growth	*The Lost*
3. A purpose	
4. An church family	

BUT FOR THIS TO HAPPEN . . .

The church must offer:

1. Compassion	
2. A plan for their lives once they are reached	*The Church*
3. A friend	
4. An altar	

BUT FOR THIS TO HAPPEN . . .

The church leadership must instill and inspire:

1. A vision to reach the lost	
2. A change of heart for the lost	*The Leadership*
3. A path to where they are	
4. A plan	

BUT FOR THIS TO HAPPEN . . .

Individual Christian men and women must undergo:

1. An awakening	
2. An intimate relationship with Christ	
3. Transformation of their hearts and minds	*You*
4. Surrender to God's ways and His thoughts, sensing the Lord calling them to the next level	

Now, let me show you how this works from the grassroots up.

Individual Christian men and women experience:

1. An awakening	
2. An intimate relationship with Christ	
3. Transformation of their hearts and minds	*A Stirring*
4. A plan	

The church leadership instills and inspires:

1. A vision to reach the lost	*A Declaration*
2. A change of heart for the lost	
3. A path to where they are	
4. A plan	

The church extends:

1. Compassion	*A Revolution*
2. A plan for their lives once they are reached	
3. A friend	
4. An altar	

Reaching the lost with:

1. Salvation	*An Outpouring*
2. A plan for growth	
3. A purpose	
4. A church family	

Can you see it? Can you see the plan, and can you see your role in the process? The main point of the plan is this: the generals can't do it without the grassroots, rank-and-file Christian, and the individual Christian can't do it alone without the covering of the church and our collective effort. The church can't do it, either, until it is willing to go places it has never gone, to reach people who don't look anything like the typical churchgoer, and to extend ourselves into areas that are altogether unlike us.

FINDING OUR VOICE

I believe that there will be such a stirring in the people of God that hundreds, even thousands of pastors and Christian leaders will sense it and hear from God. I believe ideas will arise that have never been thought of and that unprecedented alliances will begin to form that will frighten some and send others scurrying for the dark corners where gossip and slander reside. For most—for the hearing and the seeing—they will see the hand of God and come under its power and anointing and reap a harvest. World events will no longer hold ominous implications for us as we will begin to see the movement of God in every news broadcast and with each movement of the world powers.

When September 11, 2001, happened, the worst was thought about everything. The church experienced a nation searching for answers and pews filled with searchers seeking solace, hope, and information about what comes after life, but we weren't ready. We were grieving right along with them and were simply not prepared for this eventuality. Not that we were wrong for grieving, but we were wrong for praying every week to reach the lost, only to be surprised when they actually showed up.

I love the story that is told in the movie about the two farmers who went to church to pray about the drought. There had been a three-year drought. Both were just about at the end of their means, and both were desperately seeking God for rain, but when they left the service, what they did next speaks to their levels of faith. One farmer went home and continued to pray and hope for rain, but the other went home, and, despite the fact that there was not a cloud in the sky and no forecast for rain in the near future, he immediately began to prepare his fields for rain. Now, you tell me, which farmer had greater faith?

We must prepare for rain, for the latter rain, and for the multitudes in the valley of decision. We must be prepared so that when they move out of that valley and into our churches, seeking salvation, we will show them God's plan for their lives, a friend, and a reason to live.

As I write this, I am reading from an article somewhere on the back pages of a newspaper. The article is titled, "Proselytizing Pastor Jailed." It is from Tashkent, Uzbekistan. The article says that Uzbek authorities have arrested a Pentecostal Christian pastor on charges of illegal proselytizing and running an unregistered religious organization. The place where this occurred is predominately Muslim, and the official stated that the pastor "led an underground Charismatic Pentecostal church in the eastern city of Andijan and was converting Muslims to Christianity." This precious pastor now faces up to twenty years in prison for "inciting religious hatred, insulting Islam, and distributing banned literature."[1]

I read this in my suburban home at my kitchen table, while my children rest peacefully upstairs. Tashkent seems millions of miles away, but somewhere in that Muslim stronghold in some God-forsaken prison sits a precious servant of God. He is probably all alone and completely unnoticed, but, I tell you, he has *not* gone unnoticed by the God he serves, the angels, and the lives he has personally led to a saving faith. His is a dangerous faith. His is a dangerous path, a path that led him behind enemy lines to one of many valleys of decision. Blessed is his sacrifice and his suffering. Right now:

- In Africa alone there are millions of children who will grow up absent any formal family structure as millions of parents are succumbing to the deadly AIDS virus.[2]

- Every fourteen seconds a child is orphaned by AIDS.[3]

- In Sudan, millions have died in civil wars.

- In the United States, over 40 million babies have been murdered since *Roe v. Wade*.[4]

- There are 1,530,454 people in prisons in the United States, plus 4.2 million on probation and another 784,408 on parole.

- Nationwide, one in thirty-two adults is under corrections supervision, and in some states, one in fifteen adults is under corrections supervision.[5]

- There are thousands upon thousands of children in need of foster care in the United States alone. Each precious child has a soul that needs a person to stand in the gap and bring hope and salvation to them.

- Innocent men and women are dying at the hands of terrorists every day.

- Once-great churches and cathedrals in Europe now sit empty or are used as tourist attractions or other businesses.

- The worldwide drug trade is as strong as ever.

- People in many third world countries die every day from malnutrition and starvation.

- The slavery trade still exists in parts of the world.

- Millions worldwide worship false gods every day.

- Millions of people worldwide simply do not see the need for God or religion in their weekly lives.

A lie cannot live.[6]

—Martin Luther King Jr.

Praise God for the simple truth in that one great statement by a revolutionary, world-changing human being who chose a dangerous faith over the illusionary life lived with a head in the sand. A lie *cannot* live. It is like fireworks in the sky. It can seem so big and so real, even deceptively beautiful, but it ultimately burns out and ceases to exist, and it is replaced by empty sky and silence. So shall the ways of the wicked be—here and then gone, seemingly so strong—only to find out that they do not have the stuff that sustains life, only death.

There is so much to do, but we serve a "so-much" kind of God. The secret is to do your part and to play your role in your generation. The world is dying of spiritual dehydration and spiritual starvation as the soul God created cries out for its Maker.

GET ALL THE WAY IN

There it is, all spelled out in the previous pages. Who are you going to be? As God said in 1 Kings 11:38, "Then it shall be, if you heed all that I command you, walk in My ways, and do what is right in My sight, to keep My statutes and My commandments, as My servant David did, then I will be with you and build for you an enduring house, as I built for David."

Won't you come before your Father—your Creator, your best friend—and lay your life at His feet today? Won't you commit right now to being all He created you to be? Won't you surrender your right to yourself and take up your cross and follow Him? Declare it. Give it. Surrender it all to Him, and then watch what a beautiful thing He creates out of your simple act of obedience and surrender.

I leave you with these timeless words from the very God of the universe, your God, the Creator of all:

> *Now what I am commanding you today is not too difficult for you or beyond your reach.* It is not up in heaven, so that you have to ask, "Who will ascend into heaven to get it and proclaim it to us so we may obey it?" Nor is it beyond the sea, so that you have to ask, "Who will cross the sea to get it and proclaim it to us so we may obey it?" No, the word is very near you; it is in your mouth and in your heart so you may obey it. *See, I set before you today life and prosperity, death and destruction.* For I command you today to love the LORD your *God, to walk in his ways, and to keep his commands, decrees and laws;* then you will live and increase, and the LORD your God will bless you in the land you are entering to possess.... *This day I call heaven and earth as witnesses against you that I have set before you life and death, blessings and curses. Now choose life, so that you and your children may live and that you may love the LORD your God, listen to his voice, and hold fast to him.*
>
> —Deuteronomy 30:11–16, 19–20, NIV, emphasis added

There is a life to live and a mission with your name on it. It is a next-level life with a next-level purpose. It exists in a realm that cannot be seen with physical eyes and cannot be understood by human logic. It is a life of obedience, mission, and intimate relationship with Christ. A life lived at the next level is not the easy path. It leads through the very narrow way of the cross, but it is a life of incredible adventure, daring rescues, and miracles yet to unfold.

Are you in? Are you ready to do the work of preparation, sacrifice, and submission? Are you willing to lay down your life and allow Christ to be formed in you so that He might do an incredible work in you and through you? Are you ready to be poured out on the altar and shaped into something of great significance and profound meaning? If so, then tell Him exactly that.

Declare your intentions to the God of the universe, and see if all of heaven does not come and stand at your side. It will, and you will never be the same. The world He died to save will experience the very reason you were created. So get in—all the way in—and, in the immortal words of Todd Beamer on that fateful day in 2001, "Let's roll!"

NOTES

CHAPTER 1
THE PLAY IS OVER

1. Douglas MacArthur, Brainy Quote online, "Douglas MacArthur Quotes," www.brainyquote.com/quotes/authors/d/douglas_macarthur.html (accessed October 19, 2007).

CHAPTER 4
CONNECTING WITH OTHER BELIEVERS

1. Jentezen Franklin, *Fasting* (Lake Mary, FL: Charisma House, 2008), 72–73.

2. Jim Cymbala with Stephen Sorenson, *The Church God Blesses* (Grand Rapids, MI: Zondervan, 2002).

CHAPTER 7
PURIFICATION 1: THE LIGHT OF SELF-REVELATION

1. Henry Blackaby, *Experiencing God* (Nashville, TN: B&H Publishing Group, 2004).

CHAPTER 10
WILDERNESS CHRISTIANITY 1: LOVE THE LORD WITH ALL YOUR MIND

1. *Rocky Mountain News*, "Mass Experience," August 16, 1993, front page section.

2. "Each Day in America," Children's Defense Fund, November 2005, http://campaign.childrensdefense.org/data/eachday.aspx (accessed September 25, 2007).

3. Barna.org, "Spiritual Progress Hard to Find in 2003," The Barna Group, December 22, 2003, http://www.barna.org/FlexPage.aspx?Page=BarnaUpdate&BarnaUpdateID=155 (accessed September 25, 2007).

4. Richard Ross, "Youth Ministry and the Church in Ten Years," *Network* magazine, Winter 2006, National Network of Youth Ministries, http://www.youthworkers.net/index.cfm?fuseaction =netmag.viewarticle&ArticleID=141 (accessed September 25, 2007).

CHAPTER 11
WILDERNESS CHRISTIANITY 2: HOW WE KNOW THAT WE KNOW HIM

1. Chris Tomlin Interview, The FISH Atlanta, 104.7 FM, February 18, 2007.

2. Henry Blackaby, *Created to Be God's Friend: Lessons From the Life of Abraham* (Nashville, TN: Thomas Nelson Publishers, 2000), 77.

3. Darlene Zschech, *Extravagant Worship* (Castle Hill, Australia: Hillsong Music, 2001), 7–8.

4. Oswald Chambers, *My Utmost for His Highest*, February 18 (New York: Dodd, Meade, and Company, 1963).

CHAPTER 13
BUILDING YOUR SPIRITUAL HOUSE

1. Blackaby, *Experiencing God*, 24, 66–67.

CHAPTER 14
DESTINATION TRANSFORMATION

1. Rick Warren, *The Purpose Driven Life* (Grand Rapids, MI: Zondervan, 2002), 175.

2. Barna Research, "Research Shows That Spiritual Maturity Process Should Start at a Young Age," November 17, 2003, http://www .barna.org/FlexPage.aspx?Page=BarnaUpdate&BarnaUpdateID=1 53 (accessed September 28, 2007), emphasis added.

3. Abraham Lincoln, as quoted at Knox College, Larry Breitborde, "A Tradition of Innovation," http://www.knox.edu/x11885.xml (accessed October 24, 2007).

CHAPTER 15
THE HOLY SPIRIT 1: GOD'S ULTIMATE GIFT

1. Blackaby, *Experiencing God*, 37.

CHAPTER 18
DISTANCE THEORY

1. Chuck Missler, "Prelude to Tyranny: Twilight's Last Gleaming?" Koinonia House, October 2000, http://www.khouse.org/articles/2000/293/print/ (accessed October 1, 2007).

2. Ibid.

3. Twilight's Last Gleaming, Chuck Missler UPDATE from his ministry, Koinonia House, based in Post Falls, Idaho. October 2000 edition.

4. Barna.org, "Researcher Predicts Mounting Challenges to Christian Churches," April 16, 2001, http://www.barna.org/FlexPage.aspx?Page=BarnaUpdate&BarnaUpdateID=88 (accessed December 6, 2007).

CHAPTER 19
SURRENDERED GROUND

1. Chuck Colson and Nancy Pearcey, *Developing a Christian Worldview of the Problem of Evil* (Tyndale House Publishers, Inc.: Wheaton, Illinois 1999), 171.

2. Taylor Scott, The FISH Atlanta Morning Show, February 28, 2007.

3. Julie Scelfo, "Men and Depression, Facing the Darkness," *Newsweek*, February 26, 2007, 43.

4. Robert J. Foster, Tarrant Baptist Association, "Celebration of Discipline," http://www.tarrantbaptist.org/default.asp?action=getpage&page=2328 (accessed October 25, 2007).

CHAPTER 20
OUR FIXED POINT OF REFERENCE:
SOMEWHERE BETWEEN TIME AND ETERNITY

1. Chuck Colson and Nancy Pearcey, *Developing a Christian Worldview of the Problem of Evil* (Wheaton, IL: Tyndale House Publishers, Inc., 1999), 83.

2. John Hagee, *Jerusalem Countdown: A Warning to the World* (FrontLine: Lake Mary, FL, 2007), 37.

3. Corrections Supervision: Georgia Department of Corrections; U.S. Bureau of Justice Statistics; U.S. Census Bureau. All statistics are current through December 2005.

CHAPTER 21
ON HUNDRED INCHES OF RAIN:
THE AFTERMATH OF A STORM

1. Martin Luther King Jr., *A Testament of Hope,* James M. Washington, ed. (New York: HarperOne, 2003), 475.

2. Donald T. Phillips, *Martin Luther King, Jr. On Leadership* (N.p.: Business Plus, 2000), 105.

3. National Climatic Data Center, "Mitch: The Deadliest Atlantic Hurricane Since 1780," http://www.ncdc.noaa.gov/oa/reports/mitch/mitch.html (accessed December 6, 2007); The Disaster Center, "Hurricane Mitch," http://www.disastercenter.com/hurricmt.htm (accessed December 6, 2007).

4. Dr. Alan Keyes, Former Ambassador to the UN Economic and Social Council in a convocation service on the campus of Liberty University, in a speech on Tuesday, March 30, 2004, Lynchburg, Virginia.

5. Alexander Campbell, ed., *The Christian Baptist* (St. Louis, MO: Christian Publishing Company, 1889), 461.

6. Colson Nancy Pearcey, *Developing a Christian Worldview of the Problem of Evil,* 27.

7. Rebecca L. Collins, PhD, Marc N. Elliott, PhD, et. al, "Watching Sex on Television Predicts Adolescent Initiation of Sexual Behavior," *Pediatrics* Vol. 114, No. 3, September 2004, e280–e289.

8. Nancy Ayala, Mike Clark, Jacque-lyne Janssen, et al, "Real Life vs. Reel Life," *USA Today*, Wednesday, February 13, 2002, front-page section.

9. Barna.org, "Twentysomethings Struggle to Find Their Place in Christian Churches," September 24, 2003, http://www.barna .org/FlexPage.aspx?Page=BarnaUpdate&BarnaUpdateID=149 (accessed December 6, 2007).

10. George Barna, "Spiritual Progress Hard to Find in 2003," December 22, 2003, http://www.barna.org/FlexPage.aspx?Page=B arnaUpdate&BarnaUpdateID=155 (accessed October 26, 2007).

11. Henry Blackaby, "What Do You See as the Future for the United States?" speech given at the Billy Graham Training Center, Ashville, NC, May 22, 1999.

SECTION 6
FALL IN

1. Matthew Green, "The Fall of Islam," *Ministry Today*, November/ December 2006.

CHAPTER 22
HOLY DISCONTENT

1. Barna Research Group, "Barna Lists the 12 Most Significant Religious Findings From 2006 Surveys," http://www.barna.org/ FlexPage.aspx?Page=BarnaUpdateNarrowPreview&BarnaUpdateI D=252 (accessed October 9, 2007).

2. Ed Stetzer and Phillip Connoer, "Study Shows 68% Survivability Rate for Church Plants," The Church Planting Survivability and Health Study, North American Mission Board (NAMB), http://www.namb.net/site/c.9qKILUOzEpH/b.1835745/apps/ nl/content3.asp?content_id={EBFACBFF-3FA5-4FFD-A1C6-707900CE0016}&notoc=1 (accessed December 6, 2007).

3. Scott Bessenenecker, "The New Friars," *Likewise Sampler* (Westmont, IL: Intervarsity Press, 2006), 56.

4. Blackaby, *Experiencing God*, 96.

CHAPTER 23
THE BATTLE FOR THE MIND OF MAN

1. ChristianExaminer, "Barna Lists the 12 Most Significant Religious Findings from 2006 Surveys," http://www.christianexaminer.com/ Articles/Articles%20Jan07/Art_Jan07_02.html (accessed October 8, 2007).

2. Barna Research Group, "Research Shows That Spiritual Maturity Process Should Start at a Young Age," November 17, 2003. http:// www.barna.org/FlexPage.aspx?Page=BarnaUpdate&BarnaUpdateI D=153 (accessed October 8, 2007).

CHAPTER 24
THE PLAN—OPERATION:
RESCUE THE PERISHING

1. ChristianExaminer, "Barna Lists the 12 Most Significant Religious Findings from 2006 Surveys," http://www.christianexaminer.com/ Articles/Articles%20Jan07/Art_Jan07_02.html (accessed October 8, 2007).

2. Thinkexist.com, "C. S. Lewis Quotes," http://thinkexist.com/ quotes/c.s._lewis/ (accessed October 31, 2007).

CHAPTER 25
FINDING YOUR VOICE—
THE GRASSROOTS REVOLUTION

1. Judith Hayes, "John Eldridge Seeks to Rekindle Passion in the Body of Christ," *Charisma*, November 2004.

2. Erwin McManus, Catalyst Program Handout (Los Angeles: Mosaic Church, 2003).

3. Blackaby, *Experiencing God*, 102.

4. BrainyQuote, "George S. Patton Quotes," http://www.brainyquote
   .com/quotes/authors/g/george_s_patton.html (accessed October 9,
   2007).

CHAPTER 26
FINDING *OUR* VOICE

1. Felix Corley, Human Rights Without Frontiers, "Uzbek
   authorities arrest Protestant pastor on illegal proselytizing charges,"
   http://209.85.165.104/search?q=cache:qPh2TizNAG8J:www.hrwf
   .net/religiousfreedom/news/2007PDF/Uzbekistan2007.doc+led
   +an+underground+Charismatic+Pentecostal+church+in+the
   +eastern+city+of+Andijan+and+was+converting+Muslims+to
   +Christianity&hl=en&ct=clnk&cd=1&gl=us (accessed October 31,
   2007).

2. Compassion International, http://www.compassion.com/default
   .htm/.

3. Compassion International, "AIDS Orphan Ticker," http://www
   .compassion.com/default.htm (accessed December 6, 2007).

4. National Right to Life, "Quick Facts," http://www.nrlc.org/
   abortion/ (accessed December 6, 2007).

5. Corrections Supervision, Georgia Department of Corrections,
   U.S. Bureau of Justice Statistics, U.S. Census Bureau. All statistics
   are current through December 2005.

6. QuoteDB.com, "Martin Luther King Jr.," http://www.quotedb
   .com/quotes/57 (accessed October 31, 2007).

Dr. Rich is available for special events or speaking engagements, and additional Next Level products, articles, and blogs are available online.

Please visit www.RichRogers.org or www.NextLevelUniversity.org for all your Next Level needs and to book Dr. Rich at your next event!